For You

Andreas Seidl

Handover of Power

Global Version

Volume 1: Summary

Imprint

Bibliographic information of the German National Library:
The German National Library lists this publication in the
German National Bibliography; detailed bibliographic data
are available on the Internet at http://dnb.dnb.de.

© 2022 Dipl. Pol. Theodor Andreas Seidl

Cover: Christiane Ebrecht
Translation: Übersetzungsbüro Perfekt, Munich
Proofreading, production and publishing: BoD – Books on
Demand, Norderstedt

ISBN: 978-3-7568-0276-0

Acknowledgements
My thanks go to my family and friends who have made me who I am today. Special thanks to all those who supported me in writing this book. I would like to thank all my classmates, teachers, fellow students, lecturers, demonstrators, activists, colleagues, companies and countries with whom I have had the privilege of sharing the experiences from which all the ideas in this book have emerged. I would like to thank the staff of Books on Demand for their kind helpfulness. I thank the citizens of Seligenstadt for the harmony and solidarity in which I was able to write.

Table of contents

Chapter 1: Derivation

The **Purpose of the book** is formulated in the Derivation. This volume of the book describes current problems along with suitable examples and solutions and provides information about the author and for the reader. The purpose of the book is to bring about a democratic transfer of power, to organise volunteers into a newly founded party and to win elections with this party. The book is comprised of 21 volumes and can be used to create a party programme, election programme or government programme. The 21 volumes are divided up into the following topical areas: Summary, Derivation, Constitution and the Ministries of Labour, Foreign Affairs, Education, Digital Affairs, Family, Finance, Health, Infrastructure, Innovation, Integration, Justice, Media, Security, State Organisation, Barter Economy, Planned Economy, Social Market Economy and Free Market Economy. The audience for this book is humanity. The extensive and detailed information provided reduces the risk of proceeding haphazardly during the transfer of power and then subsequently acting without aim. This book aims to introduce a dynamically convertible direct, indirect and representative democracy, to establish world peace and to shape the future of humanity for the next 200 years in the United States of the World.

In the **Notes to the reader** I speak to you directly. In this summary you find out that all the chapter titles have the same name as the corresponding volumes. The words in bold have the same names as the chapters in the corresponding volume. So you know exactly where what is. If you see numbers written as numerals and not as letters, you will know that it is the people who will determine the exact number. I mainly use the masculine form, because I am man and I think it would be nice if women write in the feminine. People of all genders are the audience for my messages. Remember that I am only human, imperfect and I make mistakes. Please use the contact form on the last page to send me suggestions for improvement, join the supporters network, donate money to support the implementation or found a party yourself. I will then send you the Statutes and Party Programme in template form. The aim of the new party, called the Dynamic People's Party, is to put the plans in this book into action in your country in the follow-up to the necessary electoral successes. If you like a lot of what you read in this book then use the opportunity it gives you to make your voice heard. Have a great time doing so.

The Derivation presents **Problems, solutions and examples** for every ministry. However only the problems are summarised in this chapter. The solutions are summarised in the following chapters. Four flaws in the political system are so pivotal that they are usually responsible for causing all the other problems in the first place.

Three of the four flaws can be found in the **State organisation**. Firstly, parties that cover all areas of policy force the voter to choose the lesser evil. Voters are forced to vote for all the proposals a party makes, even if they like different proposals for different remits from several different parties. Secondly, several politicians not elected by voters stand between ruling ministers, the laws passed and the electorate. This means that voters have no chance to use their vote to reward or punish individual members or decisions made by the government. They can only be satisfied or dissatisfied with the entire government of all ministries. Thirdly, at the end of the electoral term, politicians tend to make short-term decisions which sometimes cause long-term damage for which they are no longer responsible. Voters cannot immediately hold politicians to account for their wrongdoing. Fourthly, the only economic form that exists is the neoliberal global market economy. In the absence of a global government and global jurisdiction, international anarchy exists, where the law of the richest and strongest prevails. Citizens are not at liberty to express their ideas about freedom, security, nature and technology.

An undemocratic Internet and a lack of state coordination reveal the problems with **Digital**isation. The state's elections and administration are outdated, bureaucratic and mainly conducted in analogue paper form only. User data remains unprotected on the Internet because there is no world government to protect it. Sender and recipient cannot be identified beyond doubt. Algorithms are mainly secret and can manipulate masses.

The **Media** manipulate role models and reporting because they cannot be democratically controlled. At their ideologically controlled editorial desks they abuse freedom of expression and freedom of the press. Consumers do not know the political orientation of the medium or the authors.

The problems with **Labour** policy also lie in a lumbering bureaucracy that is burdened with so many responsibilities and regularisations that entrepreneurs and state employees lose track of them all. Employees can no longer see where open job vacancies are that would suit them. Employers cannot see how many skilled workers are located where, who is looking for a new job or when and how many will finish their training. Companies have to send their data over insecure connections using insecure programmes. Only large corporations can afford to provide adequate advice, information and security, thus squeezing medium-sized enterprises out of the market. Collective bargaining agreements that negotiate wage increases that are below the inflation rate lower real wages. People work in a hierarchical system of superiors and subordinates. In subordinates, this promotes feelings of resentment or cynicism; in superiors, it promotes bossy and wrongful behaviour. The pension system is unfair to future generations because it subsidises pension benefits through taxation and because the pay-as-you-earn system is advantageous for childless individuals. Consumer protection is ineffective because consumers know less about the products than the manufacturers. Meaning that they end up buying inferior quality, environmentally harmful products or support inhumane working conditions. If consumers sustain losses, it is difficult for them to find other victims, so that they can defend themselves against the originators in a class action lawsuit. In the finance economy, hardly any opportunities exist for investors to escape the ruinous circular economy. In the finance market, they rub up against the richest investors who have additional information and expertise at their disposal. The richest are getting richer and fewer, the poor are getting poorer and more. As a result, living standards around the world remain disparate, allowing large global companies to earn more money and compound it in the financial market. The Financial Supervisory Authority lacks sufficient information about the actual state of a business and has no chance of taking action against violations in other nation states. Agriculture damages the environment and at the same time the health and security of the food supply to future generations. It clears heavily overgrown land, leaves it partially fallow, contaminates the soil with fertiliser, kills beneficial animals and plants with pesticides, produces resistant pathogens through the widespread use of medicines and fails to conduct long-term studies on genetically modified food before it is placed on the market. Monocultures, tilling and annual plants mean that less CO_2 is filtered out of the air and less water is stored in the soil.

The problem with the **Economy** is the flaw already mentioned at the beginning, that only one form of economy exists worldwide. In the neoliberal global market economy, individuals can get rich at the expense of others without the state restricting them in their freedom to do so. Small and medium-sized enterprises cannot keep up with the competition from large corporations that trade worldwide and often later become employees in one of these corporations themselves. Corporations tend to relocate to where taxes, social security contributions and occupational safety and health standards are lowest. States begin a race to the bottom for the lowest standards. Existing welfare states attract immigrants from developing countries. Social welfare itself ensures that people become used to being dependent on someone else. It costs workers a lot in taxes and contributions and results in a high number of unemployed people who are forced into low-wage jobs. The economy has become alienated from nature, creating toxic waste and making people unable to understand or repair the technology that surrounds them. Since the global economy links the money and goods cycles, economic fluctuations and corporate bankruptcies can affect whole industries, regions or even the entire world population.

The problem with **Finances** is that with their debts, states make themselves dependent on their creditors and remove from subsequent generations the scope for equal services and reforms. Countries that manage their money better are penalised because they have to compensate countries that do not manage their money so well. The tax system is so complicated that it requires tax consultants that only the rich can afford, which is why the poor pay more taxes. Many state banks provide pretty much the same services and consume more money than necessary through staff and materials. Since the financial crisis, the national central banks have been waging a currency war, devaluing their currencies and expropriating savers. The rich can protect themselves by investing money in stock markets, the poor do not have enough savings to do this. The law of the rich unleashes its enormous power on the international financial markets. The poor work in joint-stock companies, rent from them or buy their products. The resulting profits are paid out to shareholders in dividends. The rich can increasingly afford stocks and shares. They use their voting rights to lower wages and raise rents or prices in order to maximize profits. As a result, the rich get richer and the poor get poorer. Because the rich don't live in the countries of the joint-stock companies they own, they weaken local purchasing power by exporting capital.

The problems with **Innovation** lie in the market power of corporations whose position is based on outdated technologies and who prevent new technologies by lobbying against them, increasing the costs of market entry and buying up crucial patents. Professors and their studies are biased because clients only commission them when they confirm what is wanted. Researchers are not free to choose what they want to research, but have to hope for political will and funding. In their research, they then encounter bureaucratic hurdles in their path from political regulations and powers, or hierarchical hurdles from superiors who want to proliferate from their research work. From the discovery to the promotion of their ideas, inventors can only inadequately protect them. And for some, there are no intellectual property rights at all, or the registration procedure is so complicated that procedural errors make protection impossible.

The problems in **Education** come from students who are disenfranchised by teachers and the curricula. If they fail to adapt, they lose years of their lives and end up with worse employment opportunities. Teachers can only impart knowledge according to the curriculum and policy guidelines and have insufficient professional experience in the sector whose subject they teach. Educational institutions do not align their learning with transitions, making relocating between regions and the recognition of degrees more difficult. Employers and students are affected most by the curricula, but do not help to determine them.

A bureaucratic health care system and the impairment of health in favour of outdated industrial growth are problematic for the **Health** of people and the environment. Too many health insurance companies tie up money and staff in ways that make no one healthy. Successful healers fail to receive health insurance approval and healing methods are not compared in any systematic way. Certain cures are suppressed so that more money can be made from a patient. Governments react to pandemics on their own without a plan. The pharmaceutical industry, by lobbying doctors and politicians, suppresses freely available natural cures and their research. Hospitals sometimes perform more operations than required in order to pay out more in dividends to their shareholders. Pollution endangers the health of existing and future generations because companies pass on the costs of waste to the public.

Problems with **Infrastructure** are due to obsolete networks that can no longer transport additional capacities or new technologies. The exploitation of raw materials leads to a lack of the same for future generations. Rubbish is rarely recycled and is often expensive to dispose of. Real estate is so expensive that only the rich can afford it and the poor are exploited even more by the rents they are forced to pay. Finite raw materials are wasted on transportation, although there are ways to prevent this. Energy is produced with finite raw materials and also generates harmful substances. This deprives future generations of energy and burdens their lives with pollutants. Foreign missions promoting exploitation, foreign rule and terrorism in other countries give rise to problems with **Security**. With its products, the arms industry ensures destruction, preservation of power for despots and profits for shareholders at the expense of the civilian population. For police officers, the use of lethal weapons is disproportionate in the fight against unarmed criminals. Police officers are insulted and attacked without being able to effectively defend themselves and politicians misappropriate them to fight the opposition. Secret services spy on their own population and manipulate them in the interests of the government. The number of private security services is on the rise. In some circumstances these have more people in their ranks than an army or police force. Border protection is so poor that criminals can easily evade prosecution and economic migrants can drive down the level of wages in the world economy. Disaster management is so haphazard that those blighted are forced to live in uncertainty for months.

The **Justice** is peopled by partisan judges who are more in thrall of their opinions towards clients and colleagues than to the will of the people. Court proceedings are often prolonged, are not cost-effective for the state and yet still unaffordable for many citizens. The penal system with its sentences rarely leads to the desired rehabilitation effect and does not compensate the victims. It gives rise to costs for taxpayers, so that offenders end up doing even more harm to society. Legal positions are often unclear because the ministries responsible cannot draw up the corresponding criminal laws.

The problem with dealing with **Foreign Affairs** lies in the fact that anarchy reigns internationally. There is no elected government with a functioning law enforcement, and the law of the strongest or richest applies. The globalisation of the movement of goods, money and people gives the rich the opportunity to redistribute the money that belongs to the world's population to themselves. Different standards of security, taxes, wages and currencies make profits possible as long as different standards of living exist in the world. Development aid fails to equalise global living standards because it primarily serves the donor countries.

The problem with **Integration** is the unfair treatment of different nationalities, cultures and religions, which leads to envy and resentment. Dual citizenships provide more advantages and opportunities to those who own them.

Parallel societies divide the people because citizens no longer understand one another. Minorities can either dominate majorities or be excluded, depending on what the government prefers. Immigration harms employees and immigrants because it prevents full employment and diminishes wages and labour rights. Employers, on the other hand, benefit from falling costs and the state collects more taxes. Asylum seekers are placed in a state of alienated inactivity without knowing whether and how long they will be allowed to stay.

Problems often arise in **Families** because the best interests of the child are not legally formulated and young people are neglected or have nowhere to find refuge. Love, sex and marriage are made taboo, criminalised or regulated by others. Sexual self-determination is undermined by laws. Senior citizens become increasingly lonely and impoverished. Those willing to die are forced to live.

In the chapter **About the author**, I describe **My motivation** of giving courage to hopeless people to save humanity together. **My vision** is of a humanity whose organism consists of people who are like living cells. Each takes on different roles and all control each individual cell together. Politics takes over the control of the organism for the benefit of all the cells. With the democratically controlled intranet, people connect with one another to form a self-determined acting humanity. **My goal** is a form of governance with which all the persons affected agree. The persons affected should be able to convince themselves of the charisma and profile of a candidate as well as their political programme. From the programme, they should learn how the candidate would govern once elected. **My beliefs** testify to the joyfulness of experiencing one's own destiny, the courage to achieve great things in one's life, the caution against and forbearance in the face of evil, and the connection with Earth as our home. **My educational background** reveals how I pursued my idea to write this book through extensive research and my ideas diary. The knowledge I acquired at educational institutions, during national service, in internships, by pursuing my professions, and marching on demonstrations and taking part in panel discussions, I chose to know everything a government leader needs to know. Biology, French, History and Art for my A-levels, political science, social psychology, economics and human geography during my diploma's degree and social education during my master's apprenticeship equipped me with the necessary theory. Practical field studies led me to the air force as a basic conscript, to the Continental Union in Brussels as a lobbyist and reporter, to the stock exchange in Frankfurt as an editor, to citizens in my hometown as a census collector and as a private individual to conversations with right-wing, left-wing and Salafist demonstrators about their ideas. During all these experiences, I wrote down all the ideas that came to me when I thought about how to solve related problems. **My image of human beings** is basically good because I see how good-natured little children are and how they learn to adapt to a flawed system as a result of disappointment and spite. With my new approach to all political systems, I don't want to whitewash black sheep. I want to create niches for them to survive in, where they can flock to. People grow with their own responsibility, which they should acquire after the democratic transfer of power, and which they should connect with others. **My first concept from 2009** shows a summary of how far I was with the new concept at that time. I applied with it to the TV show "Ich kann Kanzler" on the German TV channel ZDF. In **My procedure** I describe the steps in my work leading from my ideas diary to this 21-volume book and when and how I incorporated the constitutions of Switzerland and the canton of Bern and the organisational charts depicting the German federal ministries and the state ministries of the federal state of Bavaria.

Chapter 2: Constitution

The **Preamble** describes that the people, in the name of humanity, the earth and the universe, adopt a constitution which regulates the assumption of responsibility for one another.

Personal rights include fundamental rights for all people as well as civil rights, political rights and social rights for nationals.

The **State organisation** includes state foundations, political parties and state personnel. It describes how and why a state is formed, how parties drive this formation of will and how politicians are elected.

The **State powers** and how they are shared and controlled are written about. Law-making for the procedures of direct, indirect and representative democracy is described separately. The exercising of law regulates the work of governments and ministries. The mediation of law describes the information and facilitation between politicians and the people. Jurisprudence establishes accountable courts and just procedures.

On **Federalism**, the basics are explained concerning the political levels of municipalities, nations and confederations of states, the rights and relationships that link them and how one level can set and exercise its own law.

The **Responsibilities** list the obligations of each of the 18 ministries. The financial regulations specify how and where the state generates which revenues and expenditures. Foreign relations describe the validity of international law and the implementation of world peace. Security is guaranteed at home by the civil defence and police, and abroad by the army. Education and research are conducted in a networked educational space. Culturally, art is promoted and state and religion are separated. In the environment and land-use planning, natural and homeland habitats are protected, as well as access to drinking water and home ownership. It describes how the state can operate undertakings, transport infrastructure and the media, how energy can be generated, transported and stored and what communication options need to be available for citizens and the organs of the press. The economy is regulated so that it can sustain the population and is safeguarded against economic fluctuations. It describes how citizens are adequately supplied with housing, work, social security and healthcare. The residence and settlement of foreigners is regulated by a quota for foreigners and by naturalisation procedures. A division is made into constitutional law, civil law and criminal law, and conditions for victims and perpetrators are laid down.

For the **Amendment of the constitution and transitional**

provisions, it describes how and when the constitution is amended in whole or in part and which provisions apply only temporarily.

Chapter 3: State Organisation

The Ministry of State Organisation is tasked with organising the state with its political structures and processes so that all state power emanates from the people. It caters for quality management at all ministries together with the Federal Moderator's Office.

State law describes the role of nationals, politicians, town halls, ministries, parties, committees, councils, constitution, quorums, votes, governments, the election of individuals and legislation, as well as ensuring state security, subsidiarity and federalism. The Ministry of State Organisation formulates these guidelines from the constitution into laws and ensures that all ministries and parties implement them. It supports their cooperation when several economic forms, ministries or levels are involved in a project. If no one feels responsible, it assigns responsibility to one or more ministries. The people decide by majority when a ministry is to be established or shut down and whether responsibilities can be transferred to other ministries. The Ministries of State Organisation, Media Affairs and Digital Affairs operate a communications system through which politicians can interact with each other and with citizens, and citizens can control the state.

As the supreme guardian of the constitution, the **State Organisation Minister**, ensures that all state institutions comply with the constitution and guarantees the fundamental rights of all citizens. The **Federal Moderator's Office** is the organ government officials, politicians, party members and citizens can turn to when they encounter problems or have suggestions concerning the state. Federal Moderators connect the right addressees, support their working together, look for common ground and compromises. If no agreement can be reached, they make the final decision.

The **State Directory** contains profiles of all the ministries and parties and their departments or party wings can form groups there. Citizens can solicit all digital state services there and search for state officials using organigrams and cast their vote for their removal from office.

The **Persons Directory** provides all citizens with a profile and they can form groups of common interests and circles of friends. All personal data that the Residents' Registration Office records on the identity card is stored here.

Liability insurance is offered for public servants and politicians, which covers civil claims resulting from negligence in office and the level of the premium is linked to the extent and frequency of mistakes made by all politicians.

Dynamic media democracy means that citizens participate in governance through various media and determine dynamically whether governance should be direct, indirect or representative, depending on their level of satisfaction. The **Theories of dynamic media democracy** describe how citizens can participate fully, partially or not at all in democratic co-determination. A dissatisfied population can elect and vote out politicians directly, draft proposals and vote on laws, spending and government decisions, or command politicians and ministries directly in an emergency. A satisfied population can become weary of elections and lend out their vote to party members or mandate councillors to take over the election of individuals, legislation and government by proxy until revoked. The procedures remain the same, but the voters change. The same applies if citizens of a municipality, nation or an international community of states desire different levels of participation or competences. This feature allows dynamic media democracy to be adapted to any common democratic state system in the world, whether the government of a city, a nation or an international community.

The **Theory of collective consciousness through media** is about citizens linking their minds through interactive state television and the intranet and making decisions together. The state then carries out these decisions.

The **Theories of social psychological adolescence** describe how similar humans and humanity are in their development and what challenges this poses for politics. Father State and

Mother Earth are raising a child called humanity. With modern means of transport it has learned to walk, with global means of communication it has learned to talk. With dynamic media democracy, it is learning to think and act for itself. At some point it will leave the parental home, colonise new planets and find friends or enemies among aliens.

The **Theory of the state as an entrepreneur** describes how similar the policies of companies and states are to dynamic media democracy. The people own the firm, the politicians take over the management and the ministries take over the production. The state has a monopoly when it comes to legislation and the use of force within its own sovereign territory. Through stable conditions, it ensures profits bought about by self-sufficient economic cycles. Municipalities are subsidiaries and other states are competitors as long as they are not made partners through common laws, authorities and ministries.

The **Theory of short chains of legitimacy** states that citizens can elect or control the processes responsible for state powers and international agreements directly, without intermediaries, coalition agreements, the secret appointment of roles or deals.

The **Goals of dynamic media democracy** are to create peace and prosperity in the nation, afterwards on Earth and then to colonise new planets. Light shows, music, dancing, drinks and food that reward people for working together to solve problems allow people to enjoy political events. Large popular celebrations take place or gifts are given out to the people involved when government aims from the electoral programme are achieved.

The **Separation of powers** ensures that no one has sole control over the law-making, executive, judicial and mediating powers. Laws are made by voting citizens, exercised by elected politicians, adjudicated by elected judges and mediated by elected directors and administrators; moreover, the powers are located in different ministries. The mediative is the fourth power of the state, which ensures that conversations take place between citizens and the state through information and questioning rounds on state television and intranet, as well as voting on voting computers.

The **Political structure** denotes which state organs there are. **Nationals** have the right to vote to determine state powers. Together as a people, they furnish themselves with a constitution and decide how their state should function and behave towards people and other countries. Citizens who are affected equally by state, corporate and cultural policies can take democratic action together to change these policies. They then act as concerned citizens and not as a community or people. Citizens are entitled to civil rights, all persons are entitled to human rights, and naturalised foreigners are given electoral and voting rights for statistical purposes.

Town halls represent the ministries in municipalities. They have an intranet café where people can use the intranet, borrow, buy and repair equipment for it, and cast their votes in voting booths on voting computers during election week.

Politicians are ministers, deputy ministers in municipality authorities and heads of key authorities who are elected and trained in their metier and can be voted out at any time. 18 **Ministries** cover all the areas required for governance. Each ministry has its headquarters including a council building in its own capital city and the authorities required for implementing their work. Ministries can also be administered communally or internationally and then relocate their capital city. Ministries of security and justice cannot be administered municipally and the constitution always applies. Ministries can be closed and new ministries established as needed, but no more than 20. Only politicians have line manager functions in the ministries. Other than that, all employees work together on an equal footing and decide on their working conditions and work schedules democratically, with the minister having the final decision-making right. Employees can make suggestions for improvements to them and publish them in the change book in the State Directory. Only citizens of the respective country can be state employees. Their salaries fluctuate depending on how well they perform their job.

There are 18 **Parties**, one for each ministry. Each party has a manifesto describing the topical area and a working group for each department from the ministry for which it is responsible. Parties put forward politicians and programmes for elections of persons, undertake opposition work in the legislative process, occupy state premises in the capital city where their ministry is located and finance themselves through taxes and donations. Each party receives the same amount of money and donations are distributed equally across all wings. Each party can have any number of **Party wings** where different opinions are represented and bills or election programmes are drafted. Prior to votes, party wings issue proclamations on how they would vote. One-day wings may exist for a short time to solve a particular problem. Citizens can be members of any number of parties and party wings free of charge. Politicians have to be members of the party as long as they are in office in the corresponding ministry. Parties support citizens to create initiatives, petitions and demonstrations or create them in the wings. All members are entitled to vote at **Party congresses**. At these conferences, government work is discussed, new proposals for laws formulated, election programmes drawn up and candidates nominated. Morally questionable pending government decisions are divided up into arguments for and against by all wings in an **Ethics commission**. Here, compromises are sought and proposals for decisions are formulated, on which citizens then vote.

Councils also exist for each ministry. They are called upon when politicians ask them for advice or citizens have lent out or given their votes to them. In councils, members of the same wings can form factions. The **Council of Ministers** comprises all deputy ministers from a ministry who have been elected in their municipality. There, municipalities coordinate government services and ensure equal supply. If citizens have given their voting rights to the council of ministers, it takes over the negotiations and votes on their behalf. The minister presides. The **International Council** is a larger council of ministers because all the municipalities from the member states take part in it. It is presided over by the International Minister. If one is not yet appointed, all national ministers share the chairmanship in turn. The **Party Council** is made up of all delegates and wing leaders, who provide their reasons at the Council for how they will vote. The Party Council only convenes therefore before the election of individuals and votes. Citizens can loan out their vote to party members, so-called delegates, so that they vote for them in certain votes. If they know each other, wishes can also be taken into account. If citizens loan out their vote to the wing leader, the vote is always made in line with the wing's proclamation. Citizens can still vote and by doing so automatically cancel the loaned out vote. The Party Council exists at municipality, national or international level. At municipality level, it replaces the Council of Ministers if citizens wish to loan out their votes to it. Citizens are free to choose which party and which level they loan out their vote to. Each party and ministry can convene a **Scientific Advisory Board**, which is made up of expert government officials servants who, together with the institutes from the ministries and universities, produce expert opinions on complicated issues.

The **Political processes** describe the procedures that take place between state organs. They dynamically adapt to the citizens' willingness to participate. Therefore, voting, elections of individuals and legislations can be direct, indirect or representative. Citizens are granted the right to vote for the Ministries of Family and Education from the age of 10 and for all other ministries from the age of 18. Naturalised foreigners are granted the right to vote in elections and referendums from the same age onwards for statistical purposes in order to be able to detect and avoid parallel societies at an early stage. These **Political rights** allow them to obtain information from any source, express their opinion freely and cast their vote unaltered. The **Right to vote** provides for voting weeks but no postal voting. Voting is held in intranet cafés or mobile voting booths. Recounts are conducted as soon as 50 per cent of those eligible to vote therefore opt-in. Election advertisements are produced in cooperation with the Ministries of Media Affairs and Digital Affairs. They are broadcast on state television and the intranet for party wings free of charge and on equal terms. Political processes take place at **Real and digital events**. Real events can include committees staged in marketplaces or council buildings. Digital events can include quorums and voting. By participating digitally in real events, any number of people can participate. The Ministries of Media Affairs and Digital Affairs do the broadcasting. They mostly use People's Motor Vehicles and People's Computers for this.

Each citizen can cast their vote once for a **Quorum**. As soon as a sufficient number of citizens do so, the quorum is formed and the corresponding political process is set in motion. A quorum has no time limit and only ends as soon as it is formed or its reason ceases. Once formed, the quorum is reset to zero votes. Voting takes place digitally over the Quorums Directory, where each quorum has a profile and supporters and opponents can create groups. When voting, citizens can provide reasons and make proposals so that politicians have a chance to bring about change before the quorum is formed. Party wings can promote voting for certain quorums as opposition work. Quorums exist for majority ratios, the creation or abolition of a quorum, the deselection and re-election of politicians, direct, indirect or representative participation, the eligibility of state personnel, the submission of a citizens' initiative, the appeal against a state decision, the repeal or amendment of a law, the revision of the constitution, people's empowerment over a ministry, the dismissal of a public servant, and for the redistribution of responsibilities between municipal, national and international levels.

The **Committee** represents a process through which people can work together to find majority decision-making options. There are standard procedures for writing texts and selecting people, as well as a voting audience and expert guests and moderators on the panel. Preliminary work is undertaken by ministries, political parties and affected citizens if they increasingly start to talk about a political issue. Preliminary coverage and broadcasting in real time takes place on government television. The venues for committee meetings include stadiums, People's Motor Vehicles setup in marketplaces and council buildings. Spectators can participate in the committee meeting with their People's Computer if they are entitled to vote. Committees have to be convened when the constitution requires it, when ministers wish or when 30 per cent of all citizens lodge an appeal through a quorum. Once a committee has been convened, it receives a profile in the **Committee Directory**, where the agenda is determined. Visitors to a committee can form groups. Visitors to the profile page can submit suggestions for decision-making options. Each committee has an initial vote where 5 options are selected from those submitted and ranked for discussion. This is followed by a news block in which multimedia education is provided on the topic. In the negotiation between the panel and the audience, up to 3 decision options become ready for implementation, which the audience then determines in the final vote. This result is put to a vote. Voting is a process by which people can make decisions together by majority.

Voting is done either by citizens and delegates in polling booths or by politicians in the council building. As soon as a majority of at least 50 per cent is found and at least 30 per cent of those entitled to vote have taken part, a vote is deemed to have been adopted. The people are entitled to vote if articles of the constitution are to be changed, laws are to be immediately ratified, long-term ties are to be entered into with other peoples, companies are to be privatised or nationalised, politicians are to be paid more or less, debts are to be incurred or money from the state treasury is to be used. The only regular vote is the **Annual budget vote** concerning the state's revenue and expenditure. Associated with it is a vote on the approval of all government decisions and the laws drafted during the previous year.

The **State governments** are formed by one or more ministers with authority for each individual case. Government decisions take the form of laws, ordinances, municipal laws, statutes, administrative regulations or service instructions. The people assume responsibility for government when they draw up their constitution and elect politicians. Ministers and their deputies assume governmental responsibility for heading the ministries. If several ministries work together, they are equal colleagues and their cooperation is guided by Federal Moderators. Citizens oversee government work via state television and the intranet and can also control it through co-determination.

The liability is assumed by politicians until citizens have voted on the decision. After that, the people as the state are liable. For decisions at municipal level, the population of the municipality is liable after the vote. Administration is taken over by public servants and institutions of the ministries within the framework of the law.

Politicians are elected in the **Elections of persons** when citizens determine the eligibility of the state office. A person can become a politician if they do not hold any other office as a politician and loans out or suspends their gainful employment for their term of office. The election of persons takes place when a politician has been voted out of office or has resigned. Parties then draw up election programmes in their wings and put them up for primary election. The 3 most popular programmes and the 10 most popular programme points in all programmes emerge from the primary election. In the programme committee, the programmes and programme items are combined into up to one programme or divided into up to three programmes, which are put to a run-off election. For each of these programmes, candidates can apply for the candidates' committee, which is designed like a casting show. After that, 2 candidates per programme are selected to compete against each other in the run-off election. The winner then receives induction by undertaking 3 internships in their future area of work during a period of 2 weeks and, if they have not already done so, completes an in-service degree in their field. Eligible voters for the election of persons are either citizens directly, delegates indirectly or councillors representatively.

The **Legislation** can also be used for all government decisions. Citizens, party members, deputy ministers and ministers have the right of initiative to submit proposals. The same applies to counter-proposals, which are voted on at the same time. In the **Legislative Directory**, proposals receive a profile and can be commented on and evaluated by users. Working groups of parties and lobbyists form groups and agree on pros and cons of the proposal. Proposals can be simulated with the Algoracle. Controversial laws have to be negotiated with citizens in a committee. Urgent laws enter into force immediately, but at the latest must be voted on at the next budget vote. Provisional laws can apply on a trial basis within a limited trial period. In order to give those entitled to vote even more scope for shaping the vote, figures are given as digits in texts which those entitled to vote can change themselves. The average or median of these figures is used in the final result of the vote. **Lobbyists** represent the interests of business and civic society in the legislative process. Any contact they have with politicians must be made public. To avoid one-sided influence, all lobbyists concerned are invited to regular meetings where they all meet together with the politician responsible and are filmed and broadcast on government television. All lobbyists receive a profile in the **Lobby Directory** and can use it to send public lobbying messages to politicians. Associations, organisations and companies that employ lobbyists form groups. Lobbyists must be members of all groups they work for. Legislation consists of an initiative that becomes a proposal in a negotiation, which is decided on in a vote. For **Indirect legislation**, ministers are entitled to vote and are jointly responsible for the negotiation with their ministry. For indirect voting, delegates are entitled to vote. For **Direct legislation**, citizens are responsible in committees. Citizens are entitled to vote for the direct vote. In addition, citizens can voice their concerns about legislation through demonstrations, petitions and citizens' initiatives. **Representative legislation** is the responsibility of deputy ministers in the Council of Ministers and International Council, and of delegates in the municipal party council at the municipal level. Councillors are entitled to vote for representative legislation. The people are responsible for **Constitutional amendments** and are entitled to vote. Any citizen can publish a constitutional initiative in the Legislative Directory, whereupon a quorum is started and counter-initiatives can be submitted. Initiatives can include new articles, amend existing ones or abolish them. At the constitutional committee meeting that follows, a bill is negotiated and a counter-bill can be introduced. Voting is compulsory in the constitutional referendum that follows. Every 50 years, the people are asked whether they want to completely revise the constitution.

Subsidiarity means that whoever can do it best is responsible. This can be individuals, families, groups of friends, clubs, companies, municipalities, nations or international associations. The citizens concerned decide via a quorum and by vote what they themselves want to be responsible for or which level of state should be responsible.

Federalism means that there is a municipal, national and international level in the state that can assume full or partial responsibility for a ministry, several ministries or all ministries. The Ministries of Security and Justice cannot be administered municipally. As soon as several levels or ministries cooperate, the Federal Moderator's Office and the Subsidiarity Agency support them. The constitution stands above all levels and ministries. Local ministries and laws only exist if the citizens living in the municipality demand it by majority vote. In that case, their regulations apply before international or national laws and ministries. Apart from that, national ministries and laws apply until the majority in the peoples concerned wish to replace them with international laws and ministries.
The responsibility for **National policy** is assumed by ministers in the capital cities and their deputies in the municipalities. The responsibility for **Global policy** is assumed by ministers from all participating states in an international union or organisation. There they unify all the laws and the peoples of the member states then elect international ministers. When all the ministries are finally ready, the states unite into a new federal state. The deputy ministers take over responsibility for **Municipal policy** by implementing their minister's guidelines in a way that suits their municipality. Municipal laws exist if the citizens living in the district decide so by a majority. Municipality ministers only exist if a majority of the citizens of the municipality want to administer the ministry concerned communally. 5,000 citizens living municipally together can form a municipality and negotiate their territory with the surrounding municipalities in a committee. The allocation of state revenue is distributed equally per citizen or in the budget vote. Municipalities can join together to form an alliance or create own cultural protection areas.

State security remains guaranteed through the identification and combating of criminality in the state system. This concerns state employees. Persons and foreign states that jeopardise state security are tackled by the Ministry of Security. Those affected can report politicians for corruption and bribery. The reward is 10 per cent of the amount of the loss. The police, Public Prosecutor's Office and the Surveillance Television act as points of contact and prosecute the offences.

Politicians and citizens enjoy **Immunity** for statements and actions that form part of a legislative process but are still punishable before it is completed. Politicians are liable with their office and, in the case of wilful disregard of the law, also with their property and freedom.

With the **Popular empowerment**, the people can, through a quorum, gain control over ministries and govern them in part or in whole, as well as hire and fire their politicians and staff. Politicians involved also face criminal proceedings for disregarding the will of the people. **Protests** mean that demonstrations have not been adequately noticed by politicians and popular discontent continues. Government television determines whether a majority or minority is protesting and the Federal Moderator organises committees to find solutions for the minority or majority. Protests involving violence are considered rioting and are broken up by the security forces.

Punitive measures for politicians are initiated following reports from citizens or the state audit services. Citizens can report wrong decisions, corruption, inaction, violations of the law or breaches of promise by a politician anonymously over an intranet portal. In a committee of enquiry, a public trial takes place against the politicians responsible and a solution is found. Citizens who are dissatisfied with a politician can cast their vote for the deselection quorum and by doing so trigger a new election. Politicians who cause harm to the people by making negligent decisions are prosecuted under civil law and brought before a committee of enquiry. Wilful criminal decisions by politicians lead to their immediate removal from power. They are not allowed to stand for election again and official business is conducted by a Federal Moderator and representative procedure.

In a **State of exception**, there is no legal basis for action by state officials, but there is an urgent need for action. All laws which are then enacted are considered urgent laws. If they need to be enacted immediately, all ministers formulate them together in the Council of Exception and at least 55 per cent of them must agree. If they have to be enacted within a week, the representative procedure is used.

In a **State of emergency**, the state or the people must act in self-defence to avert danger; they can restrict fundamental rights to do so. For a new election in a state of emergency, the deselection quorum is repeated by a compulsory public vote. Citizens take over 30 per cent of the airtime on state news broadcasts and film state or civilian failures. In the case of **War** between states, citizens elect the military commander-in-chief and establish the direction of the war in committees. In the case of **Civil war**, police are used against criminals, but allow hostile groups to duel and brawl in designated zones and offer mediation cells for reconciliation. Mayors or Federal Moderators stage committees to find compromises. In the case of **Revolt**, citizens fight the state because they want to impose their ideas upon the incumbent government. They erect barricades, occupy or block state buildings or take hostages. The police proceed in the same way as with rioting, terrorism or the mafia. Detainees appear before the committees via video-link to reveal their motives. The Federal Moderator's Office stages committees to discuss whether people's empowerment, a committee of enquiry, charges against security agencies, a petition, initiative, creation of a cultural protection area, voting for the quorum for the affected law, constitutional article or politician in question can be the solution. In the case of a **Coup**, several citizens want to take over the ministries' power to govern by force or fraud instead of through elections and ballots. If these citizens are employees of the state, the coup is referred to as a **Coup d'état**. Irrelevant with regard to the countermeasures is whether they are state employees or simply coup plotters. If power has been wrested from the state, all ministries change to municipal responsibility. All municipalities then administer themselves and organise vigilantes and counter-attacks in association. All citizens are armed. Municipalities can surrender if 65 per cent of the municipal inhabitants agree and all their weapons have been destroyed. If power has been seized in only one municipality, the military recaptures the area. If power has been seized by rigging the vote, the votes are repeated digitally using new software or on an analogue system using turnstiles in public places. The coup ends when all insurgents are arrested or have disappeared. After the coup, committees are convened as in a revolt.

For **Switching to the new system**, this party needs an absolute majority in the national parliament and, if necessary, in the second chamber, i.e. the Council of Governments of the Regions. The existing constitution is then dissolved gradually and the new constitution is drawn up according to the above procedure and all necessary laws are amended or drafted. After that, there are no more terms of office. The head of government and the president become Federal Moderators.

Chapter 4: Digital Affairs

The Ministry of Digital Affairs is tasked with facilitating the digitalisation of administration, statistics and the economy, and to protect digital data from unauthorised access and crime. For this purpose, it maintains an intranet including directories for ministries, intranet cafés and People's Computers for citizens. It runs a People's Innovation Company for the production and maintenance of digital equipment, programmes and computer games. It organises the procurement, provision, maintenance and servicing of technical equipment and software for appointment calendar and documentation services along with a digital political archive and library for all ministries. It automatically compiles business statistics, staff polls and the current state of research through statistics, and automatically forwards proposals to the state employees affected or authorised. It digitises hardcopy writings and shares forms between all ministries.

Digital law states that data from published opinions and information is freely accessible without restriction. However, authors can charge a fee for access to the data. Personal data, on the other hand, needs to be protected from unauthorised access and secured on designated data media. The originators are the owners of their data and users are obliged to inform them about its use and obtain their permission.

Digital data protection on the Internet is the responsibility of the citizen; on the intranet it is the responsibility of the Ministry of Digital Affairs. The **Access Directory** facilitates inspection and appeal by owners by means of access logs.

To combat **Digital crime**, the Ministry of Digital Affairs runs the Institute for Information Security and Cyber Defence in cooperation with the digital police and the military.

The state's **Digital administration** dispenses with paper and files its records in directories on the intranet. Data on citizens is stored on their People's Computers, backup copies and state data on the Ministry of Digital Affairs' servers. The intranet serves as a state archive and as a platform via which citizens and state employees can access all official channels. The digital service and the Intranet People's Innovation Company handle installation and troubleshooting.

The **Statistical Office** uses all the data from the ministries, citizens and businesses to link them for simulations and make predictions concerning the impact that decisions will have.

The **Digital economy** facilitates the use of the intranet by companies to store and utilise data, as well as to find real estate, goods, services, financiers, workers and customers. Contracts concluded there are notarised automatically. Legislation for the Internet is the responsibility of the Ministry of Digital Affairs.

Law enforcement on the **Internet** is carried out by the digital police. All applications for the intranet, operating systems and programmes are provided by the Peoples' Innovation Company intranet automatically in a Linux version and with public source code on the website for free download. If citizens want to move data between the Internet and the intranet or vice versa, the Ministry of Digital Affairs takes over the process, including special security measures. Knowledge from the Knowledge Directory is transferred to the Internet once a month.

The **Intranet** is an Internet at country level with its own computers, lines and programmes with open source code. **Intranet café**s exist in every town hall where citizens can go on the intranet, vote and elect officials, as well as buy and have People's Innovation Company intranet equipment repaired. The People's Computer offers a private way to access the intranet. To access it, the ID card including data verification is needed to make the intranet a highly legal place. For those who don't want that, the Internet is open.

The **People's Navigator** allows citizens to use the intranet. In the virtual world, they can conclude agreements that they put into practice in the real world, such as laws or sales. In the virtual world, the People's Navigator represents the real world as faithfully as possible. For this purpose, all existing source codes of machines and data about living beings and objects are animated and inserted into the three-dimensional satellite image of the country. Users can move around the playing field using control commands, selectively search for something, receive messages and have intranet pages displayed when they select something on the playing field. In principle, real time is simulated. However, users can also have the past or future simulated by changing the date. Users move through this playfield with avatars that look like them and can be switched to invisible. **Avatar**s can play, work, buy, sell, debate, vote, visit and converse.

Different views exist for accessing the **Directories** in which the user can organise and link all their data and contacts. All directories consist of profiles and groups via which text, images, sound, video or programmes are made shared in posts, comments, replies and ratings. Owners can copy their data between directories and hide it from certain users.

The **People's Innovation Company Intranet** produces all the cables, equipment, operating systems and programmes required for using the Intranet, such as People's Computers, voting computers and servers. It produces mainly in Planned Enterprises, is supplied with components by national companies and uses existing open source software. Over the Feedback Directory, users report problems and suggestions and vote on changes. The use of the intranet and the first People's Computer are tax-funded. Other equipment, some programmes, simulations and advertisements from companies are subject to charge. Savings on paper, printers, storage, shipping and staff cover the costs to the government.

The **People's Computer** is a tablet PC that citizens get as a gift on their 10th birthday. It only works if you insert your ID card and register your fingerprint, face and iris on the device. Owners are responsible for their device, are not allowed to open it or take it out of the country, have to take it to the intranet café if it is decommissioned, have it located by the police if they lose it, and have it audited by the Company Auditing Agency every 3 years. Numerous upgrades make the People's Computer smaller, larger or more versatile. Transparent and opaque virtual reality glasses are provided for interactive functions. For businesses, there is a cash register that automatically counts money and posts taxes.

Programmes mainly use the computing power on servers and only access the memory and input and output functions on the terminal device. The Answer Finder serves as the intranet's search engine, the swap shop serves as the marketplace and Open Leaks serves as the virtual grievance box for anonymously posting grievances. The modulator gives users the power to anonymise their data, negotiate with others, present their opinion, obtain an overview of all the directories, link sources and connect opinions. With the image generator, they can create cover images for posts, and with the indoor virtualiser, they can depict their home or company in the virtual world of the intranet.

Computer games provide entertainment for political navigation, life planning and learning. The **Avatar simulator** allows users to create different avatars and act out life paths. The **Tax game** allows taxpayers to distribute their taxes to specific government agencies and include the result in the budget vote. The **Algoracle** allows users to make predictions about the future of the nation, community, family, economy, industry or their business. It accesses the entire data set on the intranet and simulates the current and future state of reality.

The game view corresponds to the People's Navigator. If the data is sensitive, the Algoracle can only be used in the intranet café. If the results allow conclusions to be drawn about individuals or companies, the persons concerned must provide their consent prior to the simulation. Different scenarios are provided for low probabilities. Laws must be simulated before they are introduced. With the **People-controlled politician**, citizens can take over the superintendence of politicians who have been sentenced to do so or do it voluntarily. Politicians are filmed undertaking their official duties and receive instructions from users, which are voted on in real time. The game **Policy Manager** allows users to slip into the role of a party member or politician themselves. In missions, a player network is built up, problems and solutions are found, simulated and passed by a majority in a virtual election campaign. The results of the game can be transferred to the real world as a petition, initiative or counter-proposal. If they succeed there, the players participating receive points with which they can move up in the game. The **Psychotherapy game** allows users to treat themselves and complete missions based on various strokes of fate. In the game **Second earth**, data from telescopes and satellites is processed so that users can conduct virtual searches for Earth-like planets in real space. The first to discover a planet is the one after which the planet is named. The **Education game** allows users to study all the subjects offered by state educational institutions at a distance. In missions, they form study groups with other players, have to successfully complete practical exercises and exams, answer questions they set themselves or obtain a degree with their avatar. In doing so, the players use upgrades to the People's Computer, which they can borrow or buy in the intranet café. Those who pass the final virtual exam can immediately sit for a final exam at the corresponding state educational institution in the real world.

Chapter 5: Media Affairs

The Ministry of Media Affairs is tasked with informing and educating the people and enabling all those entitled to vote to have a say in the state system. Its media service handles the press and public relations work of all ministries, facilitates civil dialogue, trains or appoints a ministerial spokesperson, writes speeches and texts on request, and arranges for the organisation of conferences and events. It prevents corruption in all the ministries with Surveillance Television.

Media law is divided into the private and state press. While the people monitor the state press and influence it through laws, the private press enjoys complete **Freedom of the press**. Press must report the truth, represent a variety of views equally and authors must state their political stance. People who do not want to expose themselves in the public domain must remain anonymous. Everyone has the right to be forgotten. New and existing **Formats** such as shows, feature films, documentaries and series are given profiles in the Format Directory and enjoy legal protection. Each broadcaster is a group containing all formats that have already been broadcast.

The **State broadcasting** corporation consists of 8 broadcasters with directly elected directors, secondary channels for overlong programmes and teletext for production information, summaries and QR codes that can be scanned using the People's Computer to participate in interactive formats. The ministry is financed through taxes, advertising revenue and film productions for companies.

Its entire range of media is available in the **Media Directory**. Programmes that the broadcaster has produced and broadcast receive profiles which are stored in the group for the broadcaster. There are categories for news, documentaries, shows and movies, an editor for files that users want to upload and an algorithm that puts together a personal TV programme for the user based on their personal preferences.

Interactivity means that viewers can participate before, during and after a show. The People's Computer is turned into an extended remote control as soon as it is used to scan the QR code shown on the state television's teletext channel. Interactive shows can travel to the scene virtually using projections or a mobile studio, set up video booths in cities for passers-by to voice themselves, and allow volunteers to submit their videos. Spectators and audience guests can vote openly or secretly, answer explorative questions and voice their opinions using the audience microphone.

The state **Radio** broadcasters convert information from state television broadcasters into pure audio and use the formats of news broadcasts, discussion groups, radio plays, commentaries by or interviews with persons concerned and responsible. Users can request music over the Media Directory and paid songs are only played if advertising partners are found who are given airtime before the song is played. The music broadcasters host outdoor events where listeners with headphones dance or play sports together.

Government Television has the most interactive programme because it involves citizens in matters of government, elections and legislation. It has studios in the capital city's council buildings and a fleet of mobile studios know as People's Motor Vehicle. In its news slots it broadcasts negotiations on international treaties, lobbyist discussions, demonstrations or council meetings in real time and sums them up afterwards. Weekly summaries are broadcast in which donation drives or cooperations for the latest innovations from the Ideas Directory are advertised. Election programmes and laws are filmed in feature film format. Series are produced for longer-running news topics. Committees are filmed mainly in studio show format to allow citizens to voice their opinions. The formats are adapted to the procedures for the election of persons, legislation or ethics committees. The show "Criminal case unsolved" supports the police in their work, the show "Games room, telly and jammer" questions politicians critically, and the show "The joke's on you" offers space for political satire.

The **News Television** only broadcasts news about policy, business, culture and crime and runs throughout the day. When new reports come up, new video clips are produced and old ones are removed. The Federal Moderator presents the news. Weekly, monthly and yearly summaries are broadcast to show viewers the course of events and decisions. Another annual review takes place prior to the budget vote and only addresses the income and expenditure generated by the ministries. All broadcasts are stored in an archive system where viewers can search for videos on the same topic. News Television is present with a mobile studio at party congresses.

Local Television performs the same tasks as Government Television, only at a municipal level, and consequently consists of a large number of regional broadcasters with different catchment areas. Each municipality has a regional broadcaster on the intranet, which is run by its residents. Citizens can make feature films on their own, volunteer to be news reporters and conduct interviews on behalf of editors. They can make documentaries about their city and produce shows in which they present their city and municipal politics and discuss various pros and cons. Local Television broadcasts the most popular content from the regional broadcasters.

Parties and ministries present their work and plans on **Party Television**. During an election week, coverage predominantly focusses on the subject of voting. Ministries show what their departments, authorities and field offices are doing in documentaries. These also cover what ministries, parties and councils are doing at the moment, how governments, committees, votes and quorums work together, what strata, milieus and interest groups there are in the population, what politicians do at the weekend and what medical treatments are available. The constitution and party programmes are filmed in feature film format, and the work of the ministries is portrayed in various genres. An annual film festival selects the best feature films from all state broadcasters. Shows accompany new ministers during their induction, discuss politicians' pangs of conscience, show the most popular content from the state broadcasters from the previous week, show how words mutate in political usage and become taboo words, and promotional videos are restaged. Shows produced by individual ministries help people find jobs, find donors or collaborators for innovations, advertise think tanks, and deal with hate and how to enjoy your work. Other shows act out scenes from everyday political life with the audience in improvisational theatre performances, or all aspects of feature films are created in unison ranging from the theme to castings to the actual filming itself. The people can mandate this interactive feature film show as being compulsory if film versions of the constitution, laws, election or party programmes have been rejected as being too one-sided.

Nationwide Citizen Television is run independently by citizens who band together through the Media Directory to form editorial groups for news, documentaries, feature films or shows. They can ask for technical support from Party Television for production purposes. The viewer majority in the Media Directory decide on the programme. The most popular citizens' productions are shown. Shows feature clubs, adventures and family life, and control selected politicians like on Surveillance Television.

Surveillance Television monitors the work of politicians and ministries both unannounced and undercover. The monitoring teams are made up of reporters and camera people, inspectors from the corresponding specialist department at the Company Auditing Agency, a digital service officer, police officers, prosecutors and freelance journalists. News stories summarise the day's work performed by all the monitoring teams. Documentaries show full-length, uncut inspections. Biographical feature films portray the persons targeted. Shows present problematic inspections, violations and models of success. When committees of enquiry or critical commentaries are broadcast on state television, the shows feature participating citizens. Other shows newly investigate news from the previous week and test products from advertising.

Educational Television cooperates with companies, research and educational institutions. Learners can submit their performance records in video format. Educational Television and the Examinations Office have scripts implemented nationwide, with each educational institution filming an assigned part of the script in class. The vehicle fleet consists of mobile homes fitted out with equipment for the film crews. The latest research results are reported in the news. Curricula are visualised in the form of documentaries. These show how knowledge can be filmed using different formats, how companies can be established and managed successfully and how cycles of money and the economy work. Excerpts that answer individual questions are linked in a video encyclopaedia. Textbooks are presented in feature film format. Shows feature the papers with the best marks, the funniest, most correct and most comprehensible film adaptations of knowledge and performance records are presented in video format in a competition, while instructions on how to use materials are shown in the latest innovation lab.

Youth Television offers a programme for minors between the ages of 6 and 18 at a suitable time of day. Younger children should not watch television at all. Young people can create videos on their own or under supervision or in lessons and upload them to the Media Directory. Youth Television staff support them in the democratic creation of films. Viewers rate these videos and by doing so decide whether they are to be included in the programme. Half of the programme consists of the own productions of young people and half of the broadcaster's productions, as in the following. The news consists of good news and adaptations of the daily news into language suitable for children. Instead of advertisements, short educational videos are shown which are adapted to the learning level of the viewers. The Federal Punch & Judy Show re-enacts press conferences given by politicians. Documentaries show the developmental stages of childhood and adolescence. Older popular children's series and films are shown as feature films to offer newer generations the same treasure trove of experience. Fairy tales are read aloud, cartoons from primary schools are shown and proverbs, virtues, norms, values, traditions, philosophies and beliefs or qualities such as punctuality, charity, meticulousness and honesty are filmed. Interactive shows convey first experiences in multimedia co-determination. Experts answer questions from children and parents in a show. Nightly shows help single people find partners for love and sex.

Chapter 6: Labour

The job of the Ministry of Labour is to run the state economy efficiently and to regulate the private economy effectively and fairly. The ministry regulates labour and collective bargaining legislation for state employees, administrates all career paths and employees, the leave and sickness file and working hours with or without flexitime in part-time or full-time work in the workplace or in homeworking. It also evaluates the work performance of all ministries in conjunction with the Company Auditing Agency.

The Ministry of Labour regulates the administration of state enterprises, which are run by their ministries. **State enterprises** are authorities and state companies operated by the ministries that politicians establish in consultation with the citizens. They are built and maintained by the Ministry of Infrastructure. As far as practicable, they operate on an entrepreneurial cost-covering and profit-oriented basis. Their total profits should not exceed 10 per cent, otherwise they lower their prices. They publish all their activities in the State Directory and use them to justify their costs in the budget vote. Their employees are democratically involved in decisions, work schedules and the appointment of line managers. Collective bargaining is conducted by the policy makers responsible together with the civil service labour union. Employees take a share in the profits above the collectively agreed wages. This profit-sharing varies according to how well each employee performs. In all other respects, the same conditions apply as for Social Market Economy companies.

The **Administrative Office** administrates all state employees, buildings and equipment. It handles personnel administration digitally through the Labour Directory, which allows working hours, workplace and duties to be specified, recorded and co-determined. The ministry has a conciliation board to which employees can turn. Occupational health and safety officers serve as the Company Auditing Agency's health inspectors.

All goods and services for the civil service are procured and supplied through the **Procurement Office**. Products that are in frequent demand are put into a catalogue which citizens are also allowed to order from in order to obtain quantity discounts by buying large quantities.

The **Theory of hybrid economic systems** describes how the barter economy of the Stone Age, the planned economy of communism, the social market economy of socialism and the free market economy of capitalism are simultaneously operated and democratically controlled in one state. In basic terms a ministry exists for each form of economy and each economy allows its participants different levels of freedom and security, which are different for each person. Popular economies expand their capacities and vice versa. Unpopular forms of economy survive at least in a museum so that they can be revived at any time. Laws and taxes for businesses and currencies are different in each economic form. Property can be bought, exchanged, bestowed, fabricated or contracted and should not do harm to the environment or any uninvolved parties. The economic forms support and complement each other in a cycle, but are also capable of surviving on their own. For instance, the market economy produces waste that is consumed or valorised in the planned economy. The planned economy and the barter economy exist in zones that are primarily created in areas where there are few jobs. The planned economy provides work, social benefits and a livelihood for all unemployed nationals. In this way, the four economic forms guarantee permanent full employment.

The **Free movement between economic forms** is guaranteed by the Ministry of Labour and is possible for companies, people, goods and services. Citizens decide in favour of an economy when buying a product and choosing a job or place of residence. Citizens' Insurance ensures everyone can take their insurance benefits with them when they change. Citizens can take on the guise of consumers and entrepreneurs in several economic forms at the same time. Although companies can only be registered in one economic system, they are able to change economic systems and then have to comply with the new regulations. Goods and services can be purchased either in a multi-market, where the range consists of products from all types of economy, or in a mono-market, where only products from one type of economy are offered. Participation in the world market is only possible without restrictions for the free market economy. This avoids competition between locations for the lowest taxes and standards and the impact of global economic crises on the entire population. Customs duties also safeguard the economic forms and can be individually adjusted with regard to goods, services and companies. If one type of economy becomes a burden on another, compensatory payments or switching taxes becomes due.

Labour policy follows the strategy of providing all citizens with an education that empowers them to pursue their vocation in at least one economic system of their choice. Training courses are coordinated with the Ministries of Education and Innovation for this reason and are linked to practical work and research. The digital labour market means that citizens no longer miss out on the opportunity to find vacancies at the right time.

The **Employment Office** takes over real and digital placement in the job market. Those unable to work or impoverished old people, surviving dependents and disabled people are placed in the planned economy. Job-seekers and companies looking for workers are obliged to report their needs through the Labour Directory, where they can advise recruiters. Recruitment consultants accompany their clients from the time they find a job to the end of the probationary period or when they start a business. Further training measures are available at any educational institution or in the Social Village. When there is a shortage of skilled workers in particular, the Employment Exchange notifies the Ministry of Education of growth in vacancies for the professions concerned. The Employment Exchange organises employment fairs, where companies canvass schools for school leavers and parties for trainees, where working conditions can be compared and business partners found. Those who are not sure which occupation suits them can complete up to 12 different internships in one year and receive the minimum wage. For professions that are only viable up to a certain age, transfer agreements are arranged with suitable companies.

The **Labour Directory** is a digital platform for the establishment of companies and for the supply and demand of workers, goods, services, innovations and companies. An algorithm facilitates automated search functions and notifications. Future market situations can be simulated by an algorithm accessing all data in the matching directories. A labour programme can be used to create work schedules democratically, network machines and manage companies digitally. People, companies and innovations have profiles. People publish their CVs and employer references there. Companies run online shops. Innovations showcase their purpose and their users. Users may want innovations, such as a specific restaurant in a specific location, or a product with a specific purpose that does not yet exist. Colleagues form groups including for company sports, employers' associations, works councils or labour unions. Collective bargaining is conducted there digitally and democratically, so that everyone involved has the right to vote. With the career path planner function, people can enter occupations and periods of time when they would like to practice these occupations. They then receive automatic notifications of which educational qualifications are required, when and where a corresponding position will become vacant and where there is sufficient demand to start a business. Applications can be created automatically.

The **Enterprise policy** from the Ministry of Labour affects all the forms of economy. It regulates no working on public holidays and at least one day off a week, that workplace accidents and sicknesses are adequately avoided through the provision of protective measures and that products do not cause any damage to people or nature when they are produced, used, consumed or disposed of. Companies that produce something have to pay the disposal costs for it. These costs can be reduced or even avoided with concepts for biodegradability and complete recycling. Packaging must be made to decompose within 15 months. Companies that continue to harm people or nature with their methods of production are forced to buy permits. The price corresponds to the eradication of the damage and research into alternatives. Businesses are audited and work processes digitalised and automated to boost the economy. Employment opportunities for researchers and inventors are created. Unconditional Basic Income is paid to maintain purchasing power. Sales of key industries abroad are prevented. In the event of insolvency, the Ministry of Labour can nationalise the enterprise concerned, pay out the residual value to persons involved and agree on the further course of action in a committee together with the population. The insolvent enterprise can either be transferred to its employees, converted into a state enterprise or sold to the Social Market Economy. Optionally, its individual parts can also be leased out or auctioned off.

The **Antitrust Agency** regulates and punishes economic crimes in the individual economic forms. Violations of fair competition are punished in market economies. False labelling and charging of prices, insufficient information for customers and passing on costs to the general public are punished in all forms of economy. Punishments range from fines to professional bans, expropriation and exclusion from the domestic economy for foreign companies.

Employee protection covers all employees in companies. It regulates the handling of hazardous goods by issuing a professional licence, performing regular examinations and issuing specifications as to what must be included in employment contracts and that they have to be concluded in writing. After 12 hours of work there has to be a break of 10 hours. Loving relationships between colleagues are not to be prevented. Life partners with the same abilities are allowed to share the same workplace. Working people have at least 60 minutes twice a month to pursue a fun activity at work. Disputes about laws, labour and collective agreements between employers and employees are to be settled by the labour court. Strikes and company blockades can occur when employers are unable to reach agreement with their works council or employers' associations are unable to reach agreement with the appropriate labour unions. Agreements are democratically negotiated in collective agreements. However, democratic management is not compulsory in Barter Economy and Free

Market Economy. Agreements on performance payments for managers have to include corresponding failure payments by managers. Temporary employment agency employees earn 10 per cent more than comparable regular employees because they often have to learn the ropes in new teams. Their wages are not allowed to be touched by the temp employment agency. Guest workers have to apply or be recruited from abroad. Their placement is tied to an employment contract and can be terminated early to ensure full employment. Unlimited employment contracts with guest workers are only permitted if they are naturalised.

The **Consumer protection** ensures, that consumers can unite in consumer protection organisations to take action against unfair competition or defective products. They have access to court proceedings and the arbitration procedure, which is run like a committee by the concerned parties and the Company Auditing Agency. The Company Auditing Agency conducts consumer research by reporting examples of good and bad products supplied to them by customers and investigating them.
All goods and services are given a profile in the **Consumer Directory**. Companies inform consumers about production, price, performance and disposal. Customers can comment on and rate the products. Defective products are examined by the Company Auditing Agency and prohibited if necessary.
Consumer information standards are used by customers to compare price and performance and have to be visible on the product or at the point of sale. Prices have to be shown in the currencies of the economic forms in which the products are produced and sold. They also have to be shown in the appropriate unit of measurement, for example per kilogram.
The **tTraffic light food labelling system** shows saturated fats, simple carbohydrates and simple sugars in red, unsaturated fats and complex carbohydrates in yellow and protein, fibre, minerals, water and vitamins in green. The nutritional value is given in kilocalories per 100 grams and per item. Consumers can scan food barcodes to create a nutritional plan in the Consumer Directory, which is linked to their Health Directory

data. The origin indicator provides information on where the product and its raw materials or individual parts were produced. The **Environmental label** indicates repairable, naturally degradable or recyclable products, safe production conditions and company liability in green, artificially degradable or recyclable products, mainly safe production conditions and limited liability in yellow and non-degradable products, unsafe production conditions and no liability in red. The seal of approval is given to all domestically produced products that meet all the standards and tests from the Social Market Economy.

Basic rules for the **Finance economy** are issued by the Ministry of Labour, and special rules are decreed by the Ministries of Economy. Those who operate companies for betting on money or issue bets on financial transactions, i.e. derivatives, need a licence to do so and have to pay a levy. Those who want to sell shares in their joint-stock company through stocks on the stock exchange have to grant the shareholders democratic co-determination rights at the annual general meeting to elect, approve or discharge the board of directors and managing directors and to determine their salaries. Labour unions can buy shares to attain a voice.

The **Financial Supervisory Authority** monitors compliance with the rules for casinos, banks, stock exchanges and insurance companies. It leads the cooperation with the Company Auditing Agency and the Ministries of Security, Justice, Foreign Affairs, Digital Affairs, Finance and Market Economy. Consumers can direct complaints about these financial institutions to them.

The **Banking Supervisory Authority** sets the reserves that banks need to hold in order to be guaranteed a minimum payout to investors. It grants or revokes the license to operate a bank, checks the source code in the transaction programmes for legality, ensures that the risk is spread sufficiently across different asset classes and manages the process in the event of insolvency. Insurance Supervisory Authority do the same for insurance companies.

The state **Rating agency** is an independent authority that examines the solvency of companies and assigns grades from 1 to 9 to indicate how likely it is that payments will default. The rating agency can access Labour Directory and Antitrust Agency data, as well as data from the Company Auditing Agency and Financial Supervision Authority, and conduct its own checks. Customers pay for their work with a surcharge because they need the information to make their purchasing decisions about securities or to choose their bank or insurance company.

The **Exchange Commission** monitors the People's Stock Exchange, Ideas Stock Exchange and free exchanges operated by companies in the Social Market Economy or Free Market Economy. The Exchange Commission grants approval for securities, i.e. stocks, bonds and derivatives, and constantly audits the stock market readiness of companies. It investigates every suspicion of insider trading, quotation and market price manipulation and examines whether sales information provides investors with adequate information. Together with the Antitrust Agency, it can break up, close down or ban finance companies that have excessive power in the market from domestic trading.

Stock market readiness is given if a company is not indebted and is able to generate profits in the long term. A minimum company value or certain rate of growth in profit are not prescribed. In **Stock exchange trading**, it should be clear who owns a company. Therefore, the names of the share owners need to be reported to the Company Auditing Agency at the time of purchase. The Company Auditing Agency reports to the Minister of Labour if foreigners hold the majority of shares. Share prices are shown in three rates per share. First, the value of the company divided by the number of shares issued. Second, the price trend of the last three sales. Third, the last sale price. Joint-stock companies can switch between the Social Market Economy and the Free Market Economy or between the People's Exchange and an international exchange.

Agriculture is conducted in such a way that the population has an adequate supply and the environment is protected. Foodstuffs and renewable raw materials are only allowed to be exported if no state money has flowed into their production and there are surpluses. The Ministry of Labour offers crop failure insurance and supports farmer user groups with advisory services and in the procurement of operating materials. Innovation auditors record success models and advise farmers on how to create ecosystems for animals and plants that benefit and protect each other. Health inspectors collect and publish data on the origin, quality, production method, processing methods and environmental protection measures when using medicines, fertilisers, chemicals and genetic modifications. They identify and test limits for addictive additives and price these foods at a premium for addictive drugs health insurance, for example sugar in pizzas. Agricultural land can be purchased by farmers on a rent-to-own scheme from the Ministry of Infrastructure. Foreigners can only lease these plots of land. Mineral resources and groundwater are only allowed to be used by state enterprises so that the people can have a say in the control of consumption.

The **Food industry** runs as directly as possible between producers and consumers. This is ensured by a mail order system through the Labour Directory and Food Directory. Animals are to be kept healthy and species-appropriate, their waste disposed of by their ecosystem or keeper. Animals must be killed as quickly and painlessly as possible. Plants are not to be contaminated with toxins, fertilisers and pesticides and are to be provided for by an ecosystem adapted to their species, which protects them from pests through screening or beneficial insects and provides them with sufficient water and nutrients in a cycle. Genetically modified animals and plants are farmed shielded from the environment to avoid uncontrolled spread. To protect the climate, permaculture is practised in fields and agribusiness in factories and rooms. Conventional agriculture is gradually switched over to permaculture by the hectare since it can produce four times the volume. As soon as permaculture without tax money reaches the yields of conventional agriculture with the subsidy of tax money, the state stops making direct payments to farmers and conventional agriculture is prohibited. Organic farming can continue as a niche product, but without state subsidies.

Permaculture means to plant and colonise perennial and annual crops and farm animals in such a way that they are best adapted to the soil and the weather and sustain each other. Humans then only need to do the pruning and harvesting. Both are increasingly being performed by new harvesting robots. Almost all open-air agricultural land is being converted to permaculture, as are state-owned green spaces by the roadside or in parks, and voluntary allotment and small-animal clubs. **Indoor agribusiness** is conducted in factories where sun, water, wind and temperature differences from the environment are converted into energy. Plants grow on high shelves. Fish are bred in underground tanks. Water is treated in a cycle made up of fish and plants. Farm animals can be kept on several floors with runs, toys and hygiene rooms. Relaxing music plays at times in agricultural factories. Grow cabinets and indoor plant systems make the technology available for private domestic use. Anyone who grows food or feedstock can offer their produce over the Food Directory.

The **Forest, hunting and forestry policy** regulates the use of state forests. State forests are used for timber harvesting with harvesters that do not compact the soil. Wild animals whose populations have become too large are allowed to be hunted there. State forests are mixed forests with deadwood or are located in Barter Economy Zones, where residents manage them. Bamboo is planted in tropical summers and can grow 20 metres in 4 months, raising the water table. The **Fisheries policy** regulates the use of waterways, pumped storage reservoirs, lakes and coastal areas. Fish, seafood and aquatic plants are cultivated there in permaculture farms. Deep-sea fishing is reserved for the Free Market Economy. Gardeners, farmers, forest workers, fishermen and their customers share their experiences over the Food Directory. Universities conduct studies together with producers and research new machinery and the most productive cultivation methods.

A **Food culture** is made possible for citizens in which foods made from protein, carbohydrates, fats, fibre, vitamins and minerals cost the same. To prevent food waste, producers and consumers coordinate their orders and food is sold before its expiry date, given away or stored in accessible bins that anyone can help themselves to.

In the **Food Directory**, producers such as seed banks, farmers, restaurants or roadside nut trees are given a profile with an option for ordering or their harvest period. Each food item is allocated a group that includes producers who make it. In the consumer section, cooking recipes can be shared and a personal meal plan can be created that is tailored to and can improve physical health conditions.

The **Nutrition of the future** is one where prices drop until food is only 10% of the cost of living. Ingredients can be changed or substituted and food supplies can be subscribed to from producers. Thanks to permaculture, more can be produced than consumed, citizens can harvest by the roadside and in parks, rivers and lakes contain drinking water and the air is filtered. Agribusiness means that all animals and plants can be farmed all over the world. In times of disaster, the population is kept supplied and new planets can be colonised more easily. Specialities are available in restaurants and old food crafts are preserved in cultural protection areas.

The **Company Auditing Agency** audits and advises companies, ministries and state agencies in a similar way as the technical inspection does for cars. Companies receive information about market gaps, excessive supply or weak demand in their respective areas. To reduce staff, jobs can be found in other companies to maintain full employment. Government agencies are specifically audited to ensure that they fulfil all legal obligations, operate in an incorruptible, cost-covering and profit-oriented manner, and operate only within the scope of their responsibilities. The audit reports on state authorities are published for the people. An annual accountability report is also published, which includes all possible fines and fees for audits and consultancy.

Employees of the Company Auditing Agency come from different ministries and work at the Company Auditing Agency for only 5 years before returning to their previous jobs. They work in teams which are regularly composed anew and are previously unknown to the auditees. They work with a computer programme that automatically displays all the necessary laws and regulations, offers checklists to complete and can access all the data from other auditors and the intranet. Company Auditing Agency staff are divided into different **Departments** depending on their specialisation. **Tax auditor**s examine corporate taxes paid, tax expenditures by ministries and government contracts with private companies. **Health auditor**s check whether workers, workplaces, goods and services are deemed healthy and compatible with the environment. **Economic auditor**s check business figures, fair working conditions and compliance with the requirements of the company's respective economic form. **Technical auditor**s check consumer protection labels as well as devices and processes that they test themselves and observe during long-term studies. They award test seals once for newly approved products and regularly for measuring instruments. Once a year, they test devices from private individuals who volunteer. **Innovation auditor**s test, certify and market inventions. They use a special computer programme that searches for the latest and best solution in the Innovation Database, the Success Model Directory, Labour Directory and Ideas Directory and simulates its implementation. They support employees in submitting suggestions for improvement. They advise inventors on filing the appropriate intellectual property rights and researchers on collaborating with companies and educational institutions working in the same research field. They approve money from the Innovation Fund or Research Cost Fund and check its use. They approve temporary exemptions of the antitrust law for innovations and transformations of companies into People's Innovation Companies. **Legality auditor**s check whether companies violate corporate criminal law, constitutional law, commercial law, labour law or antitrust law and whether they adequately protect their data or themselves against sabotage. They check whether state officials, auditors and consultants adhere to procedural and confidentiality rules and whether they are incorruptible. They check whether products are counterfeited, break according to plan or whether innovations are suppressed. They enforce insolvency law and can seize property for this purpose. They perform expropriations of companies and ensure management and compensation payments or restitution to the owners. **Business consultants** receive their consulting mandate from entrepreneurs, citizens or laws. They support the completion of the projects advised by the auditors. Citizens and laws may provide for consultation to state agencies on a one-time or regular basis. Business consultants take over the interim management of companies and negotiate with the workforce in a company committee. They have a computer programme to consult which automatically outputs suggestions concerning working methods from similar successful companies and can simulate different ways of solving problems, as well as a purchasing department that can procure all necessary products. The consulting services consist of the elimination of deficiencies from the audit report, support in setting up a company, introducing innovations or success models, market and operational analyses, profit maximisation and the handling of insolvencies.

The **Audit**s take place alternately announced and unannounced or sometimes secretly in the enterprises. They include an inspection of files, the visual inspections of premises and interviews with employees and entrepreneurs using questionnaires. Enterprises are audited every 2 years, ministries and state enterprises are audited and given advice annually. Audit costs are fee-based in Barter Economy and Free Market Economy, tax-funded in Social Market Economy, Planned Economy and for state authorities. Business figures are audited with regard to cost recovery, working conditions, goods and services, and their harmlessness for people and the environment. Results and deficiencies are recorded in an audit report. Deficiencies are be corrected within a set time limit or the operating licence expires.

The auditors give brief advice on how to rectify shortcomings or improve operating procedures, and collate successful ways of working in the **Success Model Directory**. There, inventors can charge prices for the application. Companies and state agencies implementing a success model form groups and are supervised by auditors in long-term studies to see whether the model is actually successful.

The **Institute for Evaluation** designs the programmes and

questionnaires for the auditors and consultants and measures the performance and innovation of the economy.

A **Pension** is paid out to all those who have made adequate provision for it. Nationals receive a pension account from birth and have a right to retire in a retirement home in a Social Village. The Social Market Economy offers national pension insurance and the Ministries of Barter Economy and Free Market Economy leave it up to the citizens to make their own arrangements and purchase insurance. The Citizens' Insurance scheme means that all pension contributions from all economic forms can be pooled and do not lapse.

The **Retirement age** is determined by the Ministries of Health, Labour and Finance and is put to popular vote. Pensions can be drawn from this age. Those who wish to work longer can do so. The pension payment can be a monthly or a one-off payment of all the amounts saved. It can increase if the payment is made later, or decrease if only the interest earnings are paid out. Residual amounts flow into the generation account. Those who commit suicide arrange the apportionment of their pension savings in their testament.

Chapter 7: Planned Economy

The Ministry of Planned Economy is tasked with facilitating a secure and modest life for people, but one with maximum leisure time and minimum work. To this end, it runs Social Villages in the country, which are used as barracks in the event of war. Social Villages are preferably located in areas where there are few jobs or poor services.

The **Social Village government** acts on a democratic basis by its residents and forms an alliance with all other Social Villages in order to provide in mutual exchange in the division of labour. In addition to deputy ministers, the Social Village has policymakers for housing, food, clothing and hygiene who are directly elected by the residents. Plenary assemblies are held on Sundays and regulate everything that concerns the Social Village alone. Committees regulate the concerns of all Social Villages. Social Villages, businesses, clubs and houses are given a profile in the **Social Directory**. Residents can form groups to find like-minded people, negotiate, vote, select their services and simulate future developments in their Social Village. Each receives a **Social card** which they can use to record the hours they have worked and pay for services used. The residents organise themselves democratically in **Activity communities**, acquire the requisite knowledge and material, perform projects together and use the equipment from the Social Village for this purpose. General living together is marked by work performed in solidarity for the common good, a willingness to help the disadvantaged, and friendly and creative leisure activities. House communities consist of people in the same life situation who meet each other's common needs in mutual exchange and receive training and support from professionals. Social Villages are structured to include everything needed to be self-sufficient. For **Leisure**, each Social Village has an amusement park, clubs, neighbourhood festivals, open days and a place of worship open to all religions.

The **Economic policy** of the Planned Economy guarantees full employment, profits and technical progress with as much free time as possible and comprises of two fields of work. The work area that addresses basic supply provides the residents with adequate housing, food, hygiene and clothing. The work area that addresses the supply of luxuries satisfies the additional needs of the residents and enables them to set up Experimental Enterprises or Innovation Enterprises. The Social Villages exchange goods, services or work tools and suitable locations specialise in the production of certain products or operating materials. The Planned Economy supplies other ministries with products through its Planned Enterprises and receives services from other ministries in the Social Villages in return. The Planned Economy finds itself in an **Economic cycle** of goods and people with the market economies. The surplus goods in the market economy, such as bulky waste, old clothing, obsolete machines, leftover food from supermarkets and canteens are processed, used, consumed, repaired or sold back into the market economy. Residents save on working hours or earn money in this way. Unemployed people from the market economy move into the Social Village, receive compulsory hours of work for the basic supply and can train or start businesses as they wish. They leave the Planned Economy as skilled workers or entrepreneurs in the market economy.

Sustainable growth occurs because renewable raw materials are used, biotechnology is researched and Social Villages can grow or shrink. An overcapacity of 10 per cent gives the necessary leeway to respond to sudden influxes or births. If the overcapacity is used up, residents are relocated to other Social Villages which are not overcrowded. If all Social Villages are at capacity, a new one is built in a location where the population in the vicinity agrees. If the number of residents drops, areas of it are closed down. If the number of residents is too low, the workload for individuals would be too high to ensure basic services. Then entire Social Villages are leased out or sold following popular approval.

Switching between economic forms is linked to security of supply for goods, services, people and businesses. Entry fees take the form of tariffs, taxes and payments when capacity needs to be expanded. Exit fees take the form of duties or outstanding payments for services received.

The **Entrance to the Planned Economy** can be voluntary or necessarily. Necessarily means that one cannot find work in any other form of economy, is in serious debt, disabled, lonely or old and has saved too little for retirement. If only individual social benefits are required, one can commute to the Social Village for them. Life in the Social Village and social benefits are reserved for nationals, children and asylum seekers. Since not all locations offer the same work and educational opportunities, new residents can choose suitable locations in the Social Directory.

The **Move** of people, finances and businesses differs for voluntary or necessarily relocation. When people move in, the new neighbours help. Those who move in voluntarily have to do or pay for the transport themselves. Savings are moved to People's Bank accounts. Those who relocate by necessity can keep any assets that bring them money, such as renting out a flat. Entrepreneurs who move in by necessity can keep their businesses; volunteers must transfer their businesses to the Social Market Economy or Planned Economy. Those who are new to a dwelling or workplace have a 4-week probationary period to get to know their neighbours or colleagues. Those who do not like each other can switch.

An **Illegal immigrant** is anyone who does not hand in their ID at the gate before entering and collect it when leaving.

Anyone who faces **Death** or commits suicide in the Planned Economy is given a free urn burial in the cemetery tower, which also serves as a viewing platform. **Exit from the Planned Economy** is possible at any time if the working hours account is settled or benefits are paid. The old neighbours also help with moving out. The appropriate currency is required for purchasing goods outside the Planned Economy. To obtain these currencies, goods and services need to be sold from the Planned Economy. Finite commodities are only allowed to be exported in the event of a disaster.

Enterprise policy consists of democratic management, where workers elect their managers and agree on services with their customers. Health and safety at work is governed by Social Market Economy rules.

During the annual **Needs assessment**, residents decide how much they want to consume and work, or whether they want to forgo things and have more free time. In the first vote, consumers indicate what they want. In the second, employees indicate how long they have to work for it. In the third, both results are adjusted to be compatible with one another. During the year, an algorithm controls the quantities and increases the working hours when demand increases and vice versa.

All **Consumption** is recorded digitally using the social card. Those who consume 10 per cent more than stated must pay the excess or limit their consumption. Consumption by guests and visitors translates into revenue and is calculated on the basis of prior data.

Prices are expressed in working hours and converted into Social Market Economy currency, with the Note-issuing Bank determining the rate on an ongoing basis. The Company Auditing Agency measures how long it takes to mine raw materials, process them into products, distribute them and dispose of them. Added to this is the time it takes workers to be trained in the work processes, for example doctors in medical school. The time spent on training and the production time for necessary buildings and machines is added as a multiplier to the respective working hour.

The **Duty roster** is used to adjust supply to demand. It is available digitally in the Social Directory. Residents' skills are identified automatically and assigned to the appropriate jobs. All employers report which jobs they need to fill and residents select their three preferred jobs. Those who have to occupy posts even though they are not on their wish list receive bonus points for this, which they can spend in the coming year to obtain a post of their choice. Other residents can be selectively included on the duty roster, and work can be shared, exchanged or eschewed with them. All hours worked are recorded with digital time clocks and booked to the working hours account at the company. The hours worked are recorded using cash registers or via confirmation from other residents. Overtime hours bring more services as a result. As soon as they accumulate, a new job is created. There are 10 days of leave per year in basic supply and 20 days in luxury supply.

Ownership consists of personal income, communal property in the Social Villages and people's property in the ministries. Residents receive their **Income** by receiving the goods they have ordered and by being able to use all the basic supply services. If they work in luxury supply enterprises, they receive a share of the profits. Unconditional Basic Income is also paid in the Planned Economy, but 50 per cent of it has to go into retirement savings in the Planned Economy, but it is also topped up by Planned Enterprises, which distribute their profits from automation to the residents. Child benefit remains the same and facilitates a supervised life in the children's house even in the absence of parents. All earnings are posted to a resident's labour income account at the People's Bank.

In the **Work area basic supply**, residents work compulsory hours in state institutions in the Social Village, Planned

Businesses and Planned Enterprises. In doing so, they provide the basic necessities without which they could not survive. Other than that, residents have leisure time in which they can work for greater prosperity, including in the luxury supply work area.

Basic supply **Staff** are made up of beginners, experienced workers and trained professionals, and they learn from each other. Instructions are given by the one with the most experience, otherwise working on an equal footing or independently applies. All residents over the age of 6 are required to work compulsory hours. Minors receive as many weekly hours as they have years of life. Eligible work is reserved for young people, pregnant women, senior citizens, the disabled and the sick. Each week there are 2 days off work. Residents can go to a Social Village resort of their choice for 7 days a year. Customers and co-workers can assess the work in the Social Directory and report any shortcomings. Repeated shortcomings result in punitive work, punitive transfer, employment bans, rework or expulsion from the Planned Economy. Parents each receive one year of parental leave. During this time they only have to do 50 per cent of their compulsory work, but have to take part in weekly adventure and educational activities in the children's house together with their child.

Planned Businesses are housed in centres or buildings. Social service takes care of facility management and logistics. The community centre takes the form of a covered stadium for gatherings. The commercial kitchen processes all food delivered and serves it in the dining hall or as a take-away. The supply centre houses a hairdresser, kiosk, cinema, bar, discotheque and a social market. The social market supplies residents with consumer goods and donated, repaired or used goods. New goods from the Planned Economy can be ordered through a catalogue. Any goods from the market economy can be ordered in buyers' associations as soon as enough residents agree on a product and receive a quantity discount. The janitors department builds, renovates and maintains all buildings and assigns pupils to collect rubbish and residents to do sweeping duties. The laundry cleans textiles, items and buildings. The central warehouse stores consumables and machines that can be used on loan. In the workshop, residents can repair or make things.

In the **Work area luxury supply**, residents voluntarily work hours in Planned Enterprises, Experimental Enterprises, Innovation Enterprises and People's Innovation Company. This allows them to earn work hours or save money to buy goods outside of the basic supply framework, as well as start businesses, in order to leave the Planned Economy. The facilities are state-owned and consist of multi-purpose factories and office buildings. The **Staff** in the luxury supply work area consist of volunteers, shareholders and entrepreneurs who apply for jobs there, are recruited or set up together. Residents with matching skills and interests can be found through the Social Directory. When there is insufficient work, an absence of orders or closure, workers are made redundant. Wages in luxury supply consist of profit share, which is a fixed percentage negotiated in a company committee, and a bonus for particularly hard-working employees. Additional income can be earned by inventors by selling licences for innovations or successful models, or by savers at the People's or Ideas Stock Exchange.

Planned Enterprises produce goods and services for Planned Businesses, other ministries and, if secure supply permits, the market economy. Residents there work compulsory hours to produce products for basic and luxury supplies, which were requested as desired in the needs assessment, imported en masse or ordered by other ministries. Overproduction is sold to Social Market Economy enterprises or, at peak capacity, production is undertaken for Social Market Economy enterprises to generate income. Planned Enterprises are owned half by the employees and half by the state. They are set up when needed and closed when demand fails. They are bound to secrecy and loyalty when they produce weapons or computers with voting capabilities for state contracts from the Ministries of Security, Justice, Media Affairs and Digital Affairs. Planned Enterprises for agriculture, textile industry, handicrafts and location-based large-scale industry exist in every Social Village. Standard Planned Enterprises consist of the modernisation enterprise, which adapts buildings and equipment to the state of the art and the will of the residents, the clothing enterprise, which produces clothing from old clothes and tailors the look to the wishes of the residents, and the upgrading enterprise, which repairs goods from bulk waste collections if suitable and offers them in the social market.

Residents can establish **Innovation Enterprise**s if they have made an invention for which there is a gap in the market and the appropriate IP rights. Skilled workers can be found through the Social Directory or recruited from the market economy. The Company Auditing Agency's innovation auditors test the innovation and the economic auditors test the demand. Manpower, materials, advice, filing the IP right and advertising can be paid for through crowdfunding or the Innovation Fund. Each company that has once received seed money from this fund pays 5 per cent of its profits into the fund each year. As soon as the company succeeds in making sufficient profits in the market economy, it leaves the Social Village. If it is unable to do so, it is shut down and as much as possible is paid back into the fund.

People's Innovation Companies are set up in regions with few jobs and in Social Villages with suitable Planned Enterprises as suppliers and are run by the Ministry of Innovation.

Residents who have a business idea and find enough other residents to implement it can establish **Experimental Enterprise**s. Their idea is reviewed by Company Auditing Agency auditors and if sufficient demand exists in the market economy, the Experimental Enterprise is funded. Funding consists of premises in the Social Village, materials from the central warehouse and money from the Start-up Fund for operating resources that are not available in the Planned Economy. Orders for working capital are reviewed by the Company Auditing Agency and paid for through the Start-up Fund. As soon as experimental farms are able to make a profit in the market economy, they have to leave the Planned Economy. They pay 3 per cent of the profits annually into the Start-up Fund. If they do not make a profit within 3 years, they are shut down.

Research and development is performed voluntarily by residents, employees in the companies and learners in the education centre, and they earn money with it. They can combine forces to form research communities and also extend this to any Social Village and state educational institution that wishes to participate. Participants fill out questionnaires, carry out test protocols and build and test prototypes. The aim is to market as many new IP rights as possible in series in a short time or to use the Social Village as a test field for paid studies. In the education centre paid-for research assignments from the Research Directory can be completed in final papers. Residents and companies in the Planned Economy can undertake research projects directly in the education centre. It is equipped with an innovation lab and store stocked with all the equipment from the Ministry of Innovation's mobile innovation labs that is not currently in use. The innovation workshop has 3D scanners and printers, CNC milling machines, lasers, basins, ovens and specially illuminated and ventilated chambers, programmable industrial robots and various special tools in various Social Villages. The research focus of the Planned Economy is biotechnology. Animal and plant species are researched and their microbiological processes are traced, understood and reproduced in order to allow raw materials and goods to grow in a targeted manner. Each Social Village has algae batteries and biomass reactors for this purpose. Basic research is carried out in the university at the education centre. Market research is conducted using social card data and by polling employees and customers about their degree of satisfaction with production methods, goods or services. In the area of company research, new employees are asked what they noticed, good or bad after their probationary period. Employees on training courses then present the contents to their peers. Enterprises from all economic forms, institutes and universities can use the target groups sorted into residential dwellings and digital consumer data from the Social Villages to recruit and pay volunteer residents as study respondents.

The **Planned Economy economic sectors** are those required for providing basic supply and orders from other ministries. The various industries are present in all Social Villages, but some Social Villages are larger and specialise in large-scale industries in one sector. The industries include construction, food, textiles, health, energy, electrical technology, metals, chemicals, biotechnology and mineral resources. Planned Enterprises manufacture the products and education centres provide classes for the requisite skilled workers.

The **Real estate sector** consists of Social Villages with a uniform building plan. A fence made of algae batteries surrounds the village and a road runs through the middle at one end, dividing it into two halves. On the one side are residential houses, gardens, educational facilities, recreational and sports grounds. On the other, utilities right next to the road and a commercial area behind it. At the entrance is the gate and opposite it at the other end of Central Street is the fairground. Residents pay rent by working compulsory hours, businesses by providing basic supply or paying business rates.

Residential buildings have bathrooms, bedrooms and living rooms. Flats can be separate and combined, and bathrooms and living rooms can be shared. Residents in the blocks of flats all live in the same situation and democratically set themselves house rules to live by. There is one house each for single people, single parents, couples, families, senior citizens and asylum seekers. The **Hotel** has its reception at the gate and uses free rooms in the residential houses from the 10 per cent overcapacity available. Newcomers can stay there and test whether this Social Village is the right one for them. Guests can sleep at the homes of their hosts or at the hotel. Residents can stay at the hotel for up to a week if there is a dispute at home. Visitors can book a room in advance, including cleaning, bed linen and towels. All other hotel guests have to clean their rooms themselves at the end of their stay. The Social Service does the hotel management.

In the **Finance economy**, only financial services provided by the People's Bank are allowed. Experimental or Innovation Enterprises can be transformed into joint-stock companies. Then they are owned by their employees who can take their shares to the People's Stock Exchange or international stock exchanges following a majority vote once the company has left the Planned Economy. The currency in the Planned Economy is time, i.e. hours worked, which are recorded digitally on the social card and are visible on the working hours account. The Note-issuing Bank calculates the exchange rate for the currency in the Social Market Economy by comparing labour productivity per capita. The amount of money corresponds to the number of working hours available and the educational level of all residents. The value of the currency increases when the labour output per hour increases, i.e. people can afford more or have to work less. At the vending machine at the gate, visitors can exchange money for working hours as long as they remain in the Social Village. Residents can only exchange hours of work from luxury supply into money and exchange money for benefits from luxury supply. Insurance is not offered in the Planned Economy because basic welfare covers everything. Those who want to take out insurance in other economies can do so, but they have to pay for it themselves.

Residents do **Agriculture** with indoor plants in buildings, underground agri-factories, and permaculture in their gardens and open spaces in the Social Village. The nursery organises the management of open spaces and algae batteries. It also provides residents with guidance, seeds, breeding animals and hand tools for growing crops, breeding fish and raising livestock in a field, garden, room or building. A section of each garden has to be cultivated with plants or small animals which have been matched in the needs assessment. Residents raise small animals and cultivate plants during compulsory working hours and deliver them to the commercial kitchen based on a schedule. They bring medicinal plants to the health centre where they are processed into medicines. Herders keep the vegetation in the Social Village down using herds of pigs, sheep or goats and remove any windfall fruit. The algae batteries are used to grow edible aquatic plants, fish and algae for plastic production. Plant-based intoxicants such as coffee, beer or marijuana can be grown by the residents themselves, or they can have them produced industrially, when they ordered it in the needs assessment. Those who grow their own can have the intoxicant manufactured in commercial kitchens or pharmacies, and only then are they covered by health insurance for the any ill effects.

Foreign trade is only permitted if imports do not exceed exports and sufficient money has been earned to pay for the imports. Trade agreements between the Planned Economy and other economies or states must be voted on by all Social Villagers or the people. Continental social policy allows Continentals to receive social benefits in Social Villages if their member states have paid enough into the continental social funds that pay for their accommodation.

The **Tax policy** provides revenues from trade with other economic forms. This revenue comes from visitors and guests who shop or use services; VAT on imports paid for with money; corporate taxes on profits generated by exports paid for with money; sales proceeds from overcapacity; and compensation payments from market economy ministries that place the unemployed on social welfare. If all these revenues are insufficient to provide basic supply, nationwide taxes on surplus value and enterprises have to be increased. Half of all revenues earned by Planned Businesses and Planned Enterprises from foreign trade go to the budget for the Planned Economy and half to the budget for the Social Village where the service was provided. They are distributed at budget committees by the residents.

The **Social policy** guarantees assistance in Social Villages to nationals who are in social need because of old age, disability, illness, accident, unemployment, homelessness, maternity, being orphaned or widowed. This assistance can be provided in individual terms or on a permanent basis, so that those in need of help commute to the Social Village or live there permanently. Social welfare includes health care, support and protection for families and children, work for subsistence, food and housing, free education, research, development, business start-ups, information and self-administration. Those in need of help can notify the People's Protection Service via the welfare emergency number, which then takes them out of their social setting and accommodates them in the hotel in the Social Village until the further course of action has been clarified in counselling sessions.

State services are provided by the ministries in the Social Village. As many required employees as possible are residents of the Social Village and provide services during their compulsory working hours. All ministries have an office in the **Town hall**, but the plenary hall is in the community centre. The **Security centre** houses the police, fire brigade, an ATM or branch of the People's Bank and the municipal court. The **Health centre** houses a hospital, a pharmacy and doctors' surgeries for consultants. Residents and their animals can be treated there. Treatments for special cases and Immortality Health Insurance services are only provided at university hospitals. The **Leisure centre** extends across the recreation grounds at the educational institutions with their playgrounds and playing fields, a gymnasium, swimming pool, trim trail, and climbing trees to an amusement park with a Ferris wheel and various big rides in different Social Villages. Drinking water is pumped from wells by the **Energy centre**. Effluent water is treated at the sewage treatment plant, biological waste is transformed into long-distance heat and electricity in a biogas plant, and waste is incinerated. Electricity and heat are generated and stored in all buildings using sun, water and wind. In the **House for disabled people**, they are accommodated and cared as long as their families do not wish to do it themselves. In the **Children's house** all children are accommodated who do not want to or cannot live with their parents. In an emergency, parents can also place their children there for a short time. Instead of living rooms, it has playrooms, tree houses, huts and fireplaces in the garden. The cellar contains a bomb shelter for all residents in the Social Village, which is otherwise used as a disco or music room where residents are allowed to be as loud as they want at any time. The **Education centre** houses a day-care centre, primary, comprehensive and special schools and colleges. The colleges focus on the businesses at their location and not all disciplines are offered everywhere at every college.

The **Education policy** links on-the-job training with the provision of services for basic supply. Any resident can receive on-the-job training, attend any class, take any degree and teach in order to be able to share their own knowledge with others. Tests determine the level of education attained and predictions indicate vacancies in companies seeking the chosen qualification. Exchange programmes allow school children to learn about other economic forms as well. To facilitate induction for newcomers, there are training glasses that explain all the work steps.

The **Employment exchange** allows residents to take up any profession they wish, provided they are willing to attain the relevant educational qualifications, study in different Social Villages if required and attend all the faculties and companies required. Job seekers visit companies with vacancies regularly on the job bus. Alternatively, the companies present themselves at job fairs in the Social Village. Employers can watch residents at work and poach them if they wish.

The Ministry of **Media** Affairs has a radio, television and newspaper newsroom in each Social Village so that residents can publish their own news and features in the Social Directory. To this end, they are trained in the use of equipment and formats.

The shelter for **Asylum** seekers is the initial reception centre where asylum seekers stay for the first 6 months. No more than 10 per cent of the residents are allowed to be asylum seekers, all of whom speak the same language. Asylum seekers are assigned residents as sponsors who show them how to live and work in the Social Village. Interpreters are qualified teachers of the foreign language from the education centre or asylum seekers and residents who speak the same foreign language. Asylum seekers work in basic supply, learn how to build a house and receive lessons on domestic criminal law and their rights concerning residence, freedom of movement and co-determination. Asylum seekers are exposed to democratic governance during their stay in the Social Village and subsequently apply it in the Asylum Village. All digital educational content necessary is translated into the language of the asylum seekers and published on the Internet so that they can teach their compatriots how to provide basic supply after they return home.

Mobile Social Villages are composed of containers that are stored, used and maintained in accessible locations in the Social Villages. They are used when buildings are being constructed or renovated, or when disasters leave many people homeless or major company bankruptcies create mass unemployment at one location.

For **Disaster management** purposes, the Planned Economy can be used to provide basic supply in a region or the whole country. The residents rehearse these emergency plans routinely and become briefers and instructors for the rest of the population in the event of a disaster. In the event of war, all required residents change their place of residence with that of the soldiers who use the Social Village as barracks. Luxury supply is converted to a war economy.

Chapter 8: Social Market Economy

The Ministry of Social Market Economy is tasked with creating a solidarity-based, environmentally friendly and sustainable form of economy that is geared towards safeguarding social security and prosperity at home.

The **Economic policy** ensures that the Company Auditing Agency, the People's Bank and the Ministries of Social Market Economy, Education and Innovation support entrepreneurs in setting up businesses, maximising profits, and conducting research and development. Agreements are made on quantities, prices and locations through the Company Auditing Agency to avoid overproduction and to channel waste to companies that can use it. Employees, suppliers and customers benefit from audited standards, insurance, solvency and the provision of services by the companies.

When **Switching between economic forms**, companies incur entry fees that are as high as the compulsory insurance risks claimed following entry. Exit fees are only incurred if more ministry and insurance benefits are received than contributions and business taxes paid. Anyone who establishes a company in the Social Market Economy, enters into an employment contract with such a company or buys or rents its products participates in the Social Market Economy. Insurance policies in the Social Market Economy can continue through the Citizens' Insurance scheme.

The **Enterprise policy** enables the self-employed, small and medium-sized family businesses and cooperatives to enjoy the same benefits as large corporations and place more emphasis on cooperation than on competition. Their customers place more value on social and technical standards in the production of regional products. Companies are run democratically, with founders and owners not being elected by employees, whereas other managers are. Owners and employees negotiate decisions and the works constitution in the company committee, which describes the purpose and ethos of the company. Otherwise, the procedures of dynamic media democracy apply, with works councils replacing councils and labour unions and employers' associations replacing parties. Executives in the areas of research and development, purchasing and human resources, production or services, advertising and sales are considered managers. They work a 40-hour week, can work part-time and are paid no more than 3 to 8 times the average wage in the company. In times of overload, more managers are hired for the area and work as a team. To start, they have to do 7-day internships in all areas they are responsible for, collecting ideas from employees. The companies only use and create biodegradable products that last at least 15 years and are guaranteed for 10 years unless they are consumables. They fill suitable jobs with disabled people and offer children's rooms with alternating care of all employees' children by one parent. They promote friendships between employees and those who don't like each other do not have to work together all the time, as well as through trips, celebrations and company sports.

Employee protection comprises the following rules. Employment contracts can only be limited with a material reason. The notice period is 3 months. Wages are also paid on public holidays and in the event of illness. General Health Insurance compensates the loss of earnings from the 14th day of sickness. There are 30 days of vacation per year. Vacation days can be paid out to employees. Overtime is treated like vacation and counts 20 per cent more at night and at weekends. Companies with 2 or more employees have a works council. Government employees follow the guidelines of the citizens and negotiate with their responsible politicians the working methods in order to fulfil these guidelines. A working day has a maximum of 12 hours, every 6 hours a 30-minute break must be taken. As soon as overtime is incurred that constitutes a full-time position, a new appointment must be made. Jobs do not harm workers or they get compensation. The Company Auditing Agency identifies sources of danger and offers solutions.

Labour unions and employers' associations negotiate wages and working conditions in their sector in **Collective agreements**. Employees are members of their labour union for their industry, and entrepreneurs are members of the employers' association for their industry. These employers' and employees' associations can collect membership fees to buy shares in companies in their industry in order to obtain voting rights or spend them on workplace improvements. Collective bargaining is conducted in the Labour Directory and on a TV show on Government Television. All employers and employees are entitled to vote. Employees and entrepreneurs contribute their ideas and opinions to the negotiations, evaluate them and vote on them. If a majority is not achieved, a committee is convened so that the minister or the people can decide. Strikes do not occur. One umbrella organisation for each of the labour unions and employers' organisations negotiates with their counterparts in other countries to reach continent-wide or international collective agreements.

The employer and the employee regulate in the **Employment contract** what work is to be done, how and when, by whom and for how long, and what wages are to be paid for it. Employees are expected to perform their work punctually and carefully, comply with work instructions, make suggestions for improvement, keep trade secrets and not compete with their employer. Breaches result in warnings and dismissal. Employers pay wages at the beginning of the following working week. They pay equal wages for equal work, regardless of the age of the employees. Wage growth is based on the growth rate of the Gross Domestic Product for the Social Market Economy and has to be above the minimum wage set by the Minister of the Social Market Economy. Entrepreneurs do not demand more from their employees than contractually agreed. At the employee's request, companies are required to convert full-time positions into part-time positions and provide a reference for departing employees. In case of non-compliance, employees can resign without notice. Employment contracts for apprenticeships and traineeships are specified by the Ministries of Education and Social Market Economy.

Companies avoid **Insolvency**, that is, their inability to pay their debts, by holding a tax-free reserve of at least 10 per cent of the company's value and building it up when the company grows and withdrawing money when it shrinks. Moreover, insolvency insurance exists where premiums increase when business is good and vice versa. If the business closes, creditors are paid the amount of their loan without further interest, customers are paid their deposits, suppliers are paid outstanding balances and employees are paid another month's wages.

The **Economic sectors of the Social Market Economy** consist of private, state and non-profit enterprises, as well as contracts from ministries. Non-profit enterprises do not make a profit, but reduce prices, increase wages or modernise the enterprise. If supply and solvency are threatened, Company Auditing Agency auditors can get the citizens impacted to vote on agreements concerning sales territories and prices. Private educational institutions are not given curricula but only centralised final examinations and are financed by educational contributions from the students.

The **Real estate sector** is managed through the Real Estate Directory. Past anonymised tenancy agreements and building features and characteristics can be viewed here. In order to establish residential communities, purchasers or tenants can meet at a town hall event where they can find like-minded people with similar needs, attributes, skills and interests, get shown the premises and meet the vendors or landlords. Businesses showcase buildings that can be rented or sold and are taxable. For vendors, a Company Auditing Agency technical inspector inspects the property before it is sold and publishes its opinion in the Real Estate Directory. Buyers can spend 3 per cent of business taxes on alterations and renovations and are covered against local catastrophes. Tenant and landlord associations negotiate tenancy law for leases with the Social Market Economy Minister and provide legal advice to their members. Tenants and landlords can agree on further details. Landlords can terminate tenancy agreements for reasons of personal need with a notice period of 6 months, tenants without reason within 3 months. Rental prices are allowed to deviate by a maximum of 10 per cent from the median of all rental prices within a radius of 20 kilometres and are only allowed to be raised by a maximum of 1 per cent above the inflation rate per annum in the Social Market Economy. By virtue of taxed rent, buildings are insured against damage caused by storm, hail, flood, fire, lightning, mains water, temperature, gases, vapours, humidity, precipitation. Tenants are also insured against damage to fixtures and fittings caused by water, theft and fire. The janitorial service takes care of cleaning the communal areas, small repairs and brokerage activities.

The **Finance economy** only allows money to be invested in companies that meet the standards of the Social Market Economy and are owned by nationals. Trading takes place in the national currency of the Social Market Economy. The note-issuing bank calculates the exchange rate, seeks to maintain stable prices and allows for mild deflation rather than inflation. Companies pay wages in the national currency and customers can pay in the national currency of the Social Market Economy or the international currency of the Free Market Economy. Both amounts are shown as prices on products. Banks in the Social Market Economy are not allowed to invest money in weapons, food or environmentally harmful forms of production. They are only allowed to invest money in companies in the Social Market Economy, in raw materials found within the country and in currencies of the Social Market Economy and Free Market Economy which are legal forms of tender domestically. Lending for consumption purposes is prohibited. Shares and bonds in domestic enterprises can only be sold to nationals. Enterprises in the Social Market Economy can only issue debt, i.e. bonds, on the People's Stock Exchange. Interest on the debt is equal to the growth of the company through the loan. Joint-stock companies in the Social Market Economy can only issue 50 per cent of their shares on the People's Stock Exchange to nationals. The remaining 50 per cent is linked to jobs in the corporation. Employees who fill these jobs receive voting rights and dividends. Machines are not given voting rights, but distribute their dividends equally to all employees in the form of bonuses. Shareholders receive annual dividends equal to the profit share for their shares. Dividends are not paid if the corporation makes a loss, cannot exceed 40 per cent of profits, and can only increase at the same percentage as the wages of the employees at that corporation.

The **Agriculture** is comprised of small farmers who form cooperatives to share seeds, fertilisers, fodder, and machinery, and to supply food in one process ranging from sowing to processing to distribution to the final customer in a single enterprise. Farmers in the Social Market Economy are all those who have registered their business in the Social Market Economy and foreign farmers are those who only trade with the Social Market Economy and adhere to its ecological standards. All farmers are members of the farmers' union that enforces reasonable prices in trading. Farmers also maintain and manage state-owned green spaces using permaculture and are assigned a profile in the Farmer Directory. Here, customers can form groups that pay for the expansion of cultivation in the event of supply shortages and are later paid out in food. Only as many trees are allowed to be felled that can grow back, and only during the full moon or in winter. At harvest time, farmers can call on the ministry to supply food science students, Social Village residents and prisoners as harvest helpers.

All companies in the Social Market Economy can engage in **Foreign trade** as long as they abide by the following rules. Only guest workers or goods and services that are not in short supply in the Social Market Economy and are not supplied by domestic job-seekers or enterprises are allowed to be sourced from abroad. Products can only be exported abroad if their prices are not lower than local and domestic market prices. Companies in the Social Market Economy also have to comply with all the standards at overseas establishments and are audited for this purpose by the Company Auditing Agency in the overseas country.

The **Tax policy** ensures that all state benefits and compulsory insurance are included as a lump sum in the business tax. If fewer benefits are claimed on compulsory insurance, the business tax for all decreases and vice versa. Business tax is levied as a profit tax and the Company Auditing Agency, with its advisors and innovation auditors, ensures that profits are maximised.

The ministries support companies in the Social Market Economy from initial start-up to their closure with their **State services**. For their formation, companies receive advice from the town hall, a loan from the People's Bank, a market and operational analysis from the Company Auditing Agency auditors, an intranet entry and website offering information and sales functions, a complete solution consisting of insurance, digital management programmes and bank accounts from the People's Bank, and a business consultant from the Company Auditing Agency for the first 12 months.

To ensure **Profit maximisation**, an announced and unannounced audit takes place alternately every year. Using the company's digital data, the auditors determine the most successful occupancy level for all workplaces, the most favourable purchasing opportunities and trends in behaviour among customers and other companies. Any shortcomings and suggestions for improvement are compiled and coordinated with the workforce in a company committee as to how profit can be increased without having to raise prices. If the auditors or employees observe profitable and innovative ways of working, they adopt them in the Success Model Directory, test their success on an ongoing basis in studies and market them to suitable companies. Inventors set the price for this, which drops to 0 after 10 years.

Students in **Educational institutions** undertake simple work in class or in final dissertations, research projects, and seasonal overtime **and** peak periods of work for **companies**. Employers' and employees' associations incorporate the needs of companies in their sector into the curriculum. Employees can attend particular lessons for further training. Students participate in work placements in suitable companies during the holidays before starting a new subject. In on-the-job training, they alternate between companies and educational institutions. Companies can have research assignments performed in the laboratories at suitable educational institutions by volunteer students who, if they perform well, can be recruited as employees. Companies present their vacancies for work and research assignments and vacancies for trainees, young professionals and graduates at career fairs in educational institutions.

Companies are provided with **Intranet and computing power** by the Ministry of Digital Affairs. They can use the state's central data repositories and programmes for digital management, production and sales free of charge. They can have the operating programme for every machine imported and all activities and warehouses virtualised so that an algorithm can simulate the most successful profit strategy from all the data. They can also run their sales over the intranet and Internet, with the Ministry of Digital Affairs constantly encrypting and moving all data between the two networks. The Ministry of the Social Market Economy operates **Compulsory insurances** schemes for employees and owners of businesses who pay their contributions to cover costs through business tax. Persons belonging to other economic forms have to pay profit-making contributions. All persons with at least 80 per cent income from the Social Market Economy qualify for membership in the general health insurance scheme and can use all state hospitals and health centres without restriction. Parental insurance is also a form of supplementary insurance in the Social Market Economy, through which parents receive 80 per cent of their income for more than 2 years after birth and begin to repay the amounts after the payment period. Unemployment insurance gives everyone who becomes unemployed 80 per cent of their income for 12 months. This insurance also makes the compensation payments to the Planned Economy if unemployed people have to move to the Social Village. Pension insurance provides two levels of contributions for either living in shared flats with outpatient care workers or living on a cruise ship travelling around the world with a university hospital on board. Legal protection insurance covers legal fees and court costs for losing parties. Outage insurance ensures that other companies provide a service that a company cannot and later has the costs reimbursed by the company concerned. Downturn insurance only collects premiums during an economic upturn and pays them out again during a downturn.

For **Disaster management** purposes, some or all companies in the Social Market Economy may be forced to switch production, stop trading with certain countries, or work on reconstruction in disaster areas.

Chapter 9: Barter Economy

The Ministry of Barter Economy is tasked with facilitating the Barter Economy in state-owned forestry areas, where a way of life that is as close to nature and self-determined is possible without modern technology and money.

The **Economic policy** in the Barter Economy is geared to the local conditions of the Barter Economy Zone and to stone-age, medieval or modern-day levels of comfort. The inhabitants of the different Barter Economy Zones exchange goods and services with one another that are only available at certain locations, for example coasts or quarries. They receive a handbook that teaches them how to find, process and use edible, healing or useful plants, animals and rocks. Anyone who invents something new can register a corresponding IP right at the town hall. All inhabitants in a Barter Economy Zone can use the invention free of charge, others pay licence fees for it.

Comfort levels offer residents a choice of technological advances in human history to sustain themselves. Children do not have to live at low comfort levels in the forest if they do not want to. Instead, they can live in the Social Village or boarding school in the capital of the Barter Economy Zone.

Inhabitants of the **Lowest comfort level** live in huts and caves, hunt, gather, farm and raise livestock, make pottery and simple metals, defecate in cesspits, fetch water from the well, cook and heat using fire. The entrance fee is a lump sum of the Ministries of Security, Justice and Infrastructure.

Medium comfort level inhabitants live in houses with toilets, running water and windows made of glass, work as farmers or craftsmen, cook and heat with electricity, biogas or zeolite, generate electricity with renewable energy and use LED lamps to produce light. The entrance fee is the price of the lowest comfort level plus the cost of workshops in the capital city, the sewage system, sewage treatment plant and biogas plant.

Residents of the **Highest comfort level** live on the edge of the Barter Economy Zone in caravans or containers on rented pitches with connections to the electricity, water, sewage, gas and data networks. They work from home, in the field, in the Barter Economy Zone or in the capital city. The entrance fee is the price of the medium comfort level and the rental costs.

Barter Economy Zones are areas owned by the state, such as state forests and natural parks. They are mainly established in regions with little infrastructure and employment. Non-decaying items are prohibited in Barter Economy Zones. Each Barter Economy Zone has a capital city at the perimeter, is surrounded by pitches for the highest comfort level, and inhabitants live inside the Barter Economy Zone as hermits or in settlements with paved roads to the capital. Since the capital lies outside the Barter Economy Zone, no special environmental regulations apply here and all trades and working methods are permitted so that workers can commute. Settlements are serviced by mobile schools, doctors' surgeries, People's Bank branches and the People's Motor Vehicle. Small Barter Economy Zones may have fewer comfort levels and have the nearest town as their capital.

Administration of the Barter Economy Zones is voted on in committees if all Barter Economy Zones are impacted, or at an assembly if only one Barter Economy Zone is impacted. State benefits for health, education, child welfare and security are administered by the relevant ministries in city hall. Otherwise, residents basically decide on current and future developments in their Barter Economy Zone themselves. Residents are allocated a profile in the **Barter Economy Directory**, Barter Economy Zones represent groups and settlements subgroups. There, inhabitants can negotiate, vote and barter.

The highest possible number of **Inhabitants** where all raw materials can sufficiently grow back is determined by the ministry. If the capacities are exhausted, further areas are turned into Barter Economy Zones and vice versa. Only nationals can be inhabitants. When moving in, they receive lessons from inhabitants on how to live, build and provide for themselves in the Barter Economy. Habits and chattels must be naturally degradable. Guests and tourists have to register non-naturally degradable items at the town hall when entering and leaving. Residents must house and feed their guests; tourists must pay for this.

Things that inhabitants have personally made or exchanged, for example houses or clothes, are their **Property**. Everything else in the Barter Economy Zone is public property. Common goods are animals, plants, water, electricity, **Raw** materials, fuel and building **materials**. Inhabitants decide on how to exploit them in plenary assembly, and the ministry sets limits to ensure renewability.

Switching between economic forms is possible if reliability of supply and natural renewal capacity remain guaranteed. Neighbours within 100 metres of a person or business must consent to their moving in. Exit fees include all outstanding payments or considerations. Goods and services may only be imported if they are naturally degradable. They can only be exported if the necessary raw materials can be replenished quickly enough.

Enterprise policy ensures economic and contractual freedom and makes exceptions to protect the environment and renewal capacity. Contracts for services and consideration are concluded verbally and documented by video with the People's

Computer. Companies larger than medium-sized enterprises are divided up or prohibited. Wages take the form of goods and services in return. Originators are liable for damages with compensation, which is also contractually negotiated.

Disputes over such trades can be heard free of charge by the **Settlement court**, which is run by the inhabitants themselves. Those who are dissatisfied with the verdict can go to the municipal court. Traders who become insolvent have to reach an agreement on compensation with those impacted.

Environmental compatibility is ensured if everything that is exposed to the weather without protection decomposes within 100 years and everything that is decomposed can grow back in 100 years. Non-biodegradable objects in the Barter Economy Zone are registered and removed from the register after they have been disposed of or exported. Anyone who simply disposes of non-biodegradable objects in the environment will be imprisoned for polluting the environment. Company Auditing Agency inspectors carry out unannounced or classified checks to ensure compliance. Anything that can increase the speed of renewability is registered as a success model and shared with other Barter Economy Zones. If the renewal capacity is not met, the number of inhabitants is scaled down. If environmental protection laws are violated, originators are forced to leave. The plenary assembly votes on who has to leave the Barter Economy Zone or the Barter Economy.

The **Barter Economy economic sectors** facilitate stone-age or medieval life with all modern technical and health standards. **Crafts**persons transform renewable raw materials into products, the production of which is partly outsourced to manufactories. Master craftspersons train volunteers and journeymen and unite in guilds. A guild regulates the supply of raw materials, employment levels, wages, prices and sales volumes for the craftspersons in its craft. Tools and machines are shared or loaned to each other in the workshop. The workshop is open to all inhabitants and guilds have their manufactories there. Goods are stored at the wholesale market. **Trade** and shipping are undertaken by the barterers' and wholesalers' guilds in the marketplaces and barter shops in the settlements, as well as at the wholesale market in the capital. Goods are traded with and from other economic forms in the wholesale market. Shipments within the Barter Economy Zone take place using livestock.

The **Real estate sector** consists of land as public property provided by the ministry and dwellings built by the inhabitants. The location where a house can be built is shown in the Barter Economy Directory map and the neighbours within a radius of 100 metres must agree beforehand. Those who have built a house can exchange, sell or rent it out. Rent is contractually agreed with a consideration. Vacancy is allowed for a maximum of 8 weeks a year.

The **Finance economy** for banking and insurance is taken over by other ministries. Currency involves the barterer's word of honour that they be truthful about their services. Loans are promises of payment in return in the future. The People's Bank is the only bank where residents are allowed to deposit their money. Businesses run in other economic forms must have their business account with the People's Bank. Citizens' Insurance allows benefits from other insurers to be carried over to the Barter Economy.

Agriculture is practised using permaculture in fields, forests, lakes and coasts and supplies residents, craftspersons or traders. Forestry is practised by the inhabitants on behalf of the state in order to pay their taxes. They may hunt with arrows, spears, nets, traps or fishing rods.

Foreign trade takes place in the barter trade with other Barter Economy Zones and in monetary trade with market economies. International trade is only possible through the domestic market economies or in barter trade with the Barter Economy of other states.

The **Tax policy** allows taxes to be paid with prescribed goods and services that are used to provide government infrastructure, operations and employees. Businesses that collect money from other economic forms pay business taxes on it through their tax account with the People's Bank.

State services are provided by the Ministries of Security,

Justice, Health, Education, Media Affairs, Digital Affairs and State Organisation. The **Security** forces have horses and all-terrain multi-purpose vehicles. Residents receive emergency call devices on request and **Medical care** from doctors living in the Barter Economy Zone or in the capital's hospital. Treatment is provided using naturopathy so that patients can pay for their treatment in return. If the worse comes to worse, they have to subsequently go and earn money in other economic forms or refuse treatment. Children are cared for by the settlers and regularly examined and vaccinated by a paediatrician. Parents can move into the Social Village for the first two years of life. Those who are required to attend school receive their **Education** either as part-time apprentices in the guilds, in the school in the capital, in boarding school during the winter months, in comprehensive schools in surrounding villages, primary schools in the settlement or at home. They can borrow bicycles to get to school. Those who want to home-school must pass the final test at the beginning of a lesson. Those who are home-schooled have to take part in the annual central performance records and attend classes at school if their performance is too poor.

For **Disaster management** purposes in case of drought or forest fires, the inhabitants of a Barter Economy Zone can be evacuated and resettled in Social Villages or other Barter Economy Zones. From there, they organise the reconstruction. Disasters that affect the whole country and cause blackouts and outages in digital technology are managed with the help of the inhabitants of the Barter Economy Zones. They then travel the country as facilitators and teach the population how to survive living in the lowest and medium comfort levels. Children and the sick then live with the remaining residents in Barter Economy Zone and Social Villages, the rest help with the reconstruction.

Chapter 10: Free Market Economy

The Ministry of Free Market Economy is tasked with giving companies as much freedom as possible, imposing as few legal requirements as possible and levying as little tax as possible.

The **Economic policy** hardly encourages or makes demands on enterprises. The free market provides an adequate supply of goods and services when there is sufficient demand. Prices decrease when supply is greater than demand and vice versa. The Ministry of Labour enforces the necessary regulations and controls for fair competition and consumer protection, while the Ministry of Health does the same for occupational safety and environmental protection. The ability of companies to compete on the world market is crucial for economic development. Embassies and consulates under the Ministry of Foreign Affairs support the Ministry of Free Market Economy in reporting competitive conditions abroad.

The regulations on **Switching between economic forms** protect enterprises in other economic forms from the international market power of foreign enterprises and investors. Exchange rates for the different currencies as well as standards and restrictions on the exchange of companies, persons, goods and services assure this protection. The inclusion or exclusion of persons is effected through the establishment or closure of enterprises as well as through the approval or termination of employment and leasing contracts. Any enterprise belonging to other economic forms can enter the Free Market Economy and abide by its laws henceforth. Goods and services can be traded indefinitely with other states or economic forms as long as all the parties involved can consent to it and pay for it.

Enterprises can have a voice in the **Enterprise policy** by organising themselves into chambers for crafts, industry, commerce, advertising, tourism and the liberal professions and submitting requests to the Minister of Free Market Economy. In general, employers and employees, customers and suppliers regulate their cooperation themselves through contracts. Individual cases are negotiated in court and then constitute labour law for all companies in the Free Market Economy. The working conditions are determined by the employer, the employment contract, legislation and court rulings. Freedom of contract means that it is clear in the contract who agrees what with whom, that all parties consent voluntarily, and that the contract is lodged in the Labour Directory so that it can be consulted at any time and protected against unlawful changes. Companies have the duty to inform customers about any benefits and risks associated with the desired product, to label the use of genetically modified substances, to include all costs for supplying and disposing of it, to publish vacancies in the Labour Directory, to grant parents 12 months of unpaid leave after giving birth and to pollute the environment only in such a way that the initial state can be restored for the next generation. Companies are established free of charge in the Labour Directory, choose their own amount of liability and are given a company tax account with the People's Bank. In the event of insolvency, companies are to be sold in whole or in part. Owners are liable with their personal assets up to an allowance of $10,000 and shareholders up to $25,000. State payments or loans to Free Market Economy enterprises are prohibited.

Employee protection includes paying 1.5 times wages for hours worked over 40 per week. The wage level is determined by the employer and the employee in the employment contract. Payment is made at the end of the month. Leave is not paid and is only granted for family or medical reasons. Employers and employees can terminate the employment relationship at any time without reason and notice. Employees can form works councils and join labour unions. Labour unions in an industry are allowed to negotiate collective agreements with employers or their federation, collect dues for industrial action, insure wages during strikes and buy shares in the industry represented, and engage in industrial action. Share purchases facilitate the acquisition of voting rights to manage the company. Industrial action facilitates blocking public access to the enterprise and absence from work with impunity.

The **Economic sectors of the Free Market Economy** consist of manufacturing and service enterprises in various industries. Goods and services are allowed to harm informed customers, but not the unwitting. Products must be allotted a useful life or frequency of use up to which they are usable, and be repaired or refunded free of charge. Private educational institutions must participate in the central performance records.

In the **Real estate sector**, purchasers and vendors regulate home ownership in the contract of sale; tenants and landlords regulate tenancy law in the tenancy agreement. Buildings within the country are not allowed to be let by foreign companies or investors.

The **Finance economy** is mainly regulated by the Central Bank and the Note-issuing Bank of the Free Market Economy. The currency policy is taken over by a Central Bank or the world market, depending on the type of international currency chosen. If a continental currency is created as the international currency of the Free Market Economy, the finance ministers of the member states establish and manage a common Central Bank for this money market. Those who participate in the finance economy bear the risk of losing all their money. The state assumes no liability. Foreigners and domestic citizens can take majority voting rights in Free Market Economy joint-stock companies, trade shares on international stock exchanges, lend to companies and bet on rising or falling prices. Banks are not required to hold minimum reserves, but must make outstanding payments to the Central Bank in the event of insolvency and, if necessary, make their owners, customers and employees liable for them. Companies can operate stock exchanges on which shares, bonds and bets are traded and issue their own trading conditions for this. Companies decide for themselves whether and what voting rights or dividends are attached to their shares, or what the amount, term or interest payment of their bonds is. The VAT rate is levied as Customs on dividends and interest payments that flow abroad.

In **Agriculture** no government subsidies are paid. Toxins and live genetically modified plants or animals are not allowed to be released into the environment. Medicines that can also be used on humans and can produce resistant pathogens are prohibited in agriculture.

Foreign trade is regulated by trade agreements with the states concerned. Employees at a company with several establishments in different countries can join together in a labour dispute if the labour unions cooperate. Uncriminal and debt-free guest workers can be employed if their wages allow them to live self-sufficiently. Their employment contracts are limited to 3 years or unlimited once the guest worker is naturalised. They are not allowed to remain unemployed for longer than 3 months. The guest worker may bring their family if they are naturalised and employed for an indefinite period and can pay the living expenses for all family members. Family members who are not naturalised have to leave as soon as all family members are of age. Employment contracts can be terminated without notice by the Ministry of Free Market Economy if the migrant worker becomes indebted, if they or one of their family members commits a criminal offence, or if the quota of foreigners is exceeded.

The **Tax policy** stipulates a sales tax for companies, which is levied on all payments into the company account. Tax rates can be adjusted based on industry or business size. This revenue must be adequate to pay for all tax-funded services to Free Market Economy businesses. Government contracts are awarded to Free Market Economy enterprises only if there are no comparable enterprises in the Social Market Economy or Planned Economy.

State services can be paid for with taxes or fees for individual services, subscriptions or insurance. State electoral, legislative and governmental procedures, information about them in the state media, tools for democratic corporate governance and benefits provided by the Ministry of Family Affairs including child benefits are tax-funded. Government services for which fees are payable are voluntary or required by law. The Ministry of Labour charges fees for job placement through the Employment Exchange and examinations or advice from the Company Auditing Agency. The Ministry of Foreign Affairs charges fees for country analyses for approving the import and export of capital, goods, services and guest workers. Compensation payments for the unemployed are collected by the Ministry of Planned Economy. Regular contributions are due to participate in the Ministry of Social Market Economy's unemployment insurance and pension schemes. The Ministry of Education charges fees for the education and training required by companies. The Ministry of Finance charges for analyses of countries and goods to determine customs duties. The Ministry of Health provides health insurance. The Ministry of Infrastructure charges for the connection to and use of road, rail, data, electricity, sewage and water networks and grids, as well as for selling or renting through the Real Estate Directory. The Ministry of Innovation charges educational institutions or innovation labs fees for research contracts. The Ministry of Integration charges the companies concerned for integration measures for guest workers and their dependents. The Ministry of Digital Affairs charges for the use of the intranet for sales or administration purposes and for transferring the content of intranet pages to company websites. The Ministry of Justice charges lawyers' fees and court costs, collects contributions for legal protection insurance or wage payments for prisoners as employees. The Ministry of Security charges companies for security services provided by the People's Protection Service or the fire brigade.

Chapter 11: Finance

The Ministry of Finance is tasked with generating revenue by levying taxes and generating profits, which it spends in consultation with the people. It stabilises the value of money with the Central Bank and citizens can increase their savings in their economy with the People's Bank. Its salary office takes care of the salary, expenses, travel and relocation costs for state employees.

The **Theory of the state as a company** enables citizens to profitably manage their state like a democratically run enterprise. Citizens are thereby consumers, owners and workers in equal measure. They operate an economic cycle through state services, innovation and various economic conditions that generate profits and tax revenues. A low suicide rate, birth rates between 2 and 3 children per woman, and an educated and affluent population with a high life expectancy keep the economy stable and profitable in the long run.

The **Tax Office** collects taxes and administers the revenues and expenditures of all ministries. It saves the revenue in the People's Bank for the coming year's budget.

The **Tax policy** provides for the digital collection of taxes by diverting them through tax accounts. Each taxpayer is given a tax account with the People's Bank and a profile in the Tax Directory. Taxes are levied as a percentage to charge all payers in the same ratio.

Value added tax (VAT) is levied on every outgoing transfer and cash withdrawal from private accounts. Its rate is the same in all forms of economy. Private services with consideration are handled and taxed through the People's Computer.

Business taxes are levied on every inbound transfer to business accounts and on cash receipts with special cash registers. Everyone who generates money with a business must register a company and open a company account, including shareholders. Both can be done free of charge and automatically over the Labour Directory and People's Bank. The tax rates are different in all economic forms and hence represent the plethora of state benefits that companies expect to receive there. Sales taxes are levied in the Free Market Economy and Barter Economy, profit taxes in the Social Market Economy and Planned Economy. In order to harmonise economic conditions between the economic forms, an exchange tax may be introduced at times.

Tariffs represent a tax on foreign trade. They control trade with developing countries by making goods and services that are detrimental to those countries more expensive. They raise the price of trade with countries that fail to respect environmental and human rights. Additionally, they offset losses in VAT and strongly positive or negative foreign trade balances.

Taxes on assets are levied to reduce government debts accrued for previous generations. They are levied on inheritance, gifts and annually on land until the debt is reduced. **Tax reduction** is achieved by financing government services through fees and adding a maximum of 10 per cent profit to the cost-recovery price of these services. People's Innovation Companies generate monopoly profits in world trade until the IP right expires. State assets are invested for profit.

The **Unconditional Basic Income** is linked to the level of automation. Machine fees amount to 50 per cent of the savings between human and machine labour and accrue as soon as a machine has yielded its purchase price. Half of them go into a fund for automation and half into a fund for the Unconditional Basic Income. Payment to citizens begins as soon as the returns on the Unconditional Basic Income fund allow for an amount of $100, which then increases steadily. As soon as 80 per cent automation is achieved, the machine fees are cancelled and the money in the automation fund is invested profitably. 20 per cent of this interest revenue goes back into the automation fund and 80 per cent into the Unconditional Basic Income fund. The citizens decide how high the share of corporate taxes on automated enterprises should then be.

Budget consolidation means running the state budget without debt, reducing existing debt and building up profits. Municipalities and economic forms offset each other's surpluses and losses. If losses have to be made up, the budget vote decides whether countermeasures or permanent compensation payments are to be adopted on the basis of regional specifics. The Ministry of Finance saves all state revenues in order to use them in the next budget period or to set them aside to cover economic downturns or reforms. If debts exist abroad, they are rescheduled. Balances in citizens' current and instant access savings accounts with the People's Bank are used or government bonds are sold to citizens and interest is paid at the rate of inflation or the Gross Domestic Product growth rate. Income from interest is not supposed to flow abroad, but to boost domestic purchasing power.

For **Debt reduction** the Ministry of Finance works out plans with citizens containing measures for debt reduction that apply for a certain period of time. For example, 3 holidays per year for 5 years can be cancelled in order to repay five-year government bonds with these revenues. By **Balancing the business cycles** surpluses are saved in upturns, which are distributed again in downturns.

State revenues consist of taxes, fees for government services, invested state revenues generating income from interest and dividends, licences for inventions made by state institutions, and profits from marketing government services provided by the authorities and People's Innovation Companies. In exceptional cases, debt can also be incurred if the people agree and sufficient citizens deposit their money in People's Bank accounts or buy government bonds.

State expenditure is determined annually between the ministries and citizens for the coming fiscal year, which begins on the July 1st. By then, all ministers consolidate the financial plans from their ministries into a draft budget, reduce costs in consultation with citizens in a budget committee, campaign for their projects or the change in the basic amount, and let the people make the final decision in the **Budget vote**. Voters then have the opportunity to reject, amend costs or reduce funding for each individual cost centre or entire projects, authorities, units, departments or ministries. The basic amount first needs to be distributed so that the government services required by law can be provided. After that, the project amount is auctioned off. Projects represent new ventures undertaken by the state or reforms. The most popular projects among the people receive funding.

Citizens can prepare these decisions throughout the year in the **Tax game** and use their scores as a template for their budget vote. The game allows fee payers and taxpayers to allocate all of their personally paid taxes and profits from fees to the state agency of their choice.

The **Audit Court** audits state revenue and expenditure, publishes its data, can appeal against state expenditure to the Budget Committee and hears citizens' concerns that expose government wasting.

The **Central Bank** is the bank of the four note-issuing banks and the People's Bank. It controls the constant, slightly fluctuating growth of the economy in the country by issuing money. It ensures price stability and full employment. Prices that rise or fall by 1 per cent per annum are deemed stable. Full employment is considered achieved when unemployment is between 0 per cent and 2 per cent.

The **Tools of the Central Bank** operate between economic

forms and on the world market. Through its sole right to issue banknotes, no Note-issuing Bank can become insolvent. If the level of debt is too high, a vote can be convened. Exchange rates are set in consultation with the four Note-issuing Banks. If necessary, shares and bonds issued by domestic companies and government bonds issued by Continental Union member states can be bought with newly printed money to increase the money supply. These are then sold again to decrease the money supply. Currency reserves are formed from transactions conducted at the key interest rate and hedge the currencies. When the desired value is reached, the proceeds flow into the national budget. If the currency or the country is in danger, the Central Bank can release the reserves so that the citizens have a valuable means of payment.

Note-issuing Banks are the bank of banks for their economic form and can be more or less dependent on their Ministry of Economy. In the Barter Economy, the Note-issuing Bank ensures a wide supply of goods and services without surpluses or shortages. The currency consists of honour and consideration. In the Planned Economy, it makes sure that productive work is performed per hour and that as much free time as possible is provided with sufficient supplies in accordance with the duty roster. The currency in the Planned Economy consists of digitally stored hours of work and training. The Social Market Economy allows its national currency up to 2 per cent price increases and uses its instruments in consultation with the Minister of the Social Market Economy. The national currency has the same name as the last currency valid only for this country. The Note-issuing Bank in the Free Market Economy predominantly focuses on price stability and is only bound by the directives of the Central Bank. The international currency is either a precious metal, a cryptocurrency, US dollars, or a continental currency.

The **Tools of the Note-issuing Banks** are used to reduce sharp fluctuations in economic conjuncture, thereby protecting their currencies. When banks borrow money from the note-issuing bank, they pay the issue base rate for it. When they deposit money there, they pay the deposit base rate if banks lend too little, or they receive income on interest if more has been lent in total than deposited by all banks. The key interest rates set the price of money. The minimum reserve ratio controls the money supply. It indicates how much of their investors' money banks are allowed to lend out or have to hold in reserve in order to be able to pay out at least this amount to their customers in the event of a crisis. By buying or selling foreign currencies, Note-issuing Banks can influence the exchange rate for their currency.

The **Living Standard Index** determines the population's level of satisfaction by means of statistical indicators such as price level, Gross Domestic Product, unemployment, productivity, income, investment, innovation, wealth distribution, educational achievement, self-sufficiency, informal work, housework, care, DIY, volunteering, club membership, partnerships, divorces, births, suicides, friendships, life expectancy, sick days, crime, personal freedom, social services, rule of law, intergenerational equity, circular economy, global prosperity and peacekeeping.

The **Determination of the Gross Domestic Product** in all economic forms is adapted to their conditions, but always takes into account the development in production, consumption and income over the course of months and years. The price level is calculated from the development and use of the money supply, the comparison between the Gross Domestic Product of the previous months and years as well as with baskets of all goods whose price is digitally retrievable and collected and compared by an algorithm. Innovations are automatically displayed because there are no comparative prices for them yet.

The Central Bank, in cooperation with the Note-issuing Bank affected, takes **Measures in the event of inflation or deflation. Inflation** refers to an increase in prices, which can be prevented through a charge on money transactions, loans to increase production levels, obligations to stockpile, cheaper alternative products, increases in business tax and payments through the Unconditional Basic Income, automation at full employment, and independence from foreign goods. **Deflation** refers to a fall in prices, which can be prevented with a payment for money transactions, government contracts paid for with government bonds, raising VAT and paying out to industries with falling wages and prices, increasing taxation on securities, advising and lending to invest in innovation, lending by the People's Bank without interest, increasing the Unconditional Basic Income, spending on citizens' preferred projects, raising tariffs, giving early notice of drops in government spending, devaluing the domestic currency or leaving a currency group.

The **People's Bank** offers bank accounts for citizens, businesses and the government. Citizens and businesses can place their money there, but they don't have to. The state is obliged to maintain all its accounts with the People's Bank and conduct its foreign trade transactions through it. Citizens and businesses that want to change economic form must do so through the People's Bank, so that the People's Bank exists in every economic form. Account management is free, there is a network of branches throughout the country and a page on the intranet. All deposits are 100 per cent secured by the currency reserves. The **Citizen account** includes a current account which pays no interest, but which is directly available. It also includes a tax account for settling value added taxes, an daily deposit account as a government bond with an interest rate the same as the inflation rate, a savings account for investments with the People's and Ideas Stock Exchange, a pension account with $5,000 start capital at birth with an interest rate equal to the Gross Domestic Product growth rate. At retirement, the interest income is paid out, and at death, the $5,000 is repaid. Also included is a generation account, which can only be paid into. However, interest income can be withdrawn from this account as a wage subsidy or pension for the whole family. Children receive a children's account at birth for child benefit payments. Companies receive a **Company account** when they are established. It includes a current account, a tax account for business tax and a savings account to access the Ideas Stock Exchange and the Research Cost Fund, the income from which has to be invested in the business. Each ministry is given a **State account** to make its payments through the current account and to invest its income from profits in the savings account.

At the **People's Stock Exchange** nationals can buy shares, i.e. company shares with voting rights and profit sharing, or bonds, i.e. loans with a fixed term and fixed interest, from nationals' companies and resell them between themselves. Foreigners and foreign companies do not participate in order to hedge domestic purchasing power. Domestic government bonds are first sold on the People's Stock Exchange and earn interest at the previous year's Gross Domestic Product growth rate. Only if they do not find enough buyers there can they be offered on international exchanges, after the people have agreed. Any ministry can offer government bonds, for example there are real estate bonds from the Ministry of Infrastructure for the housebuilding programme.

On the **Ideas Stock Exchange** inventors sell their products or intellectual property rights in whole, part or under licence. Savers and companies can buy innovation bonds to lend inventors money for commercialisation, buy innovation shares to share in the extra profit from the innovation, buy licence-share shares to receive a share of the royalties, or buy product shares to receive a share of the royalties for an innovative, expensive product.

The **Risk** describes the probability of losing all or part of one's money, or increasing it greatly. It is lowest on the People's Stock Exchange when investing there in Social Market Economy companies or the state because they are insured against non-performance or non-payment. The Company Auditing Agency and the Securities and Exchange Commission provide the requisite information for investors. The highest risk is to be found in innovation shares whose term is expiring for upholding the intellectual property right.

Investors in the People's Bank can also invest small amounts in various **Funds**. The People's Fund is a mixed fund consisting of sub-funds for shares, bonds and indices. Companies in an industry or all companies with the highest stock market value are listed in indices. Shares or bonds are bought from the money from all investors. Either an algorithm automatically buys from all companies in an index, or a fund manager from the People's Bank selects the most profitable companies for a fee. The real estate fund can be linked to a building society savings plan and yields an owner-occupied home from the housebuilding programme. The domestic funds consist of sub-funds for shares and bonds listed on the People's and Ideas Stock Exchange. They are not allowed to exceed 10 per cent of the total volume. Units in domestic funds can be sold to foreigners.

The **Investment Department** creates algorithms for the automated investment of money, manages the funds from the People's Bank and the money saved from the treasury. Stock market games at universities identify and recruit the most capable graduates.

Chapter 12: Innovation

The Ministry of Innovation is tasked with ensuring that there are more innovations in the country and that they are marketed faster and more successfully. **Innovation cycles** give mankind its research and development. Currently, this is information technology. It has culminated in the digitalisation of the state and the automation of the economy. The following innovation cycle is to be biotechnology, which has its climax when stable self-sustaining ecosystems can be established and materials and machines are provided by biotechnologically bred organisms. Through the **International innovation policy**, countries agree on an innovation cycle and research and develop it in a division of labour in constant exchange. Each country does what it does best.

The **Innovation Agency** ensures the smooth flow from the development of an idea through marketing to the expiry of the property right. It connects appropriate authorities, inventors, companies and investors. In its innovation offices in the city halls, inventors can have a search carried out to find out whether the idea already existed or not. New ideas can be registered there and also marketed with a profit share of 20 per cent.

The Ministry of Innovation's policy for **Research and development** connects basic research, applied research and industrial research. All citizens have the right to conduct research and researchers have the scientific freedom to research anything as long as it does not pose a risk to people or the environment. Research institutions in the country form a community to share and collaborate. This involves schools, researching companies and institutes. In the **Research Directory** research projects are published in profile form in order to find researchers, sponsors and producers. In the Research Cost Fund, companies can pool their research expenses and invest in joint research projects or research projects set up by inventors or researchers. The Ministry of Innovation creates and funds **State research projects** for urgent research questions of national interest. The natural sciences research technical implementation, the social sciences research social implementation and the humanities research personal implementation. Urgent projects involve the circular economy, digitalisation, the transformation of energy and transport to use renewable raw materials and energies, which are digitally networked to achieve a higher yield with less expenditures and effort. Future-oriented projects encompass biology, the Universe and basic research that can produce biodegradable products and ecosystems on Earth and other planets through a comprehensive understanding.

Innovation through education takes place reciprocally. The Company Auditing Agency's innovation auditors gather requirements for innovation in companies, pass them on to the Innovation Agency, which arranges for them to be developed at suitable educational institutions. Young learners in particular are inventive and have imagination, which is stimulated by a suitable curriculum and research tasks in the interest of society as a whole, which no one has previously tackled. Inventions developed at state educational institutions are immediately protected under the appropriate intellectual property right. Companies are given the invention and subsequently pay the development costs to the educational institutions and licence fees to inventors while retaining a share in the profits. Inventors who are not members of an educational institution can research and develop collectively in the People's Innovation Company Think Tank after classes are over. Inventors who lack the necessary expertise can attend all the required events at the universities. Volunteer researchers are trained in mobile innovation labs to explore government research projects.

The **Technology policy** is intended to test, authenticate, standardise and commercialise new technologies in goods, services, workflows and digital systems. The Institute of Technology sets out the procedures for this, which are conducted by Company Auditing Agency examiners. Appropriate **Industrial property rights** are granted for all innovations, namely patent, design, copyright, trademark and industrial process. The **Patent Office** is responsible for compiling, granting and renewing industrial property (IP) rights. It reports promising patents which may form the basis for a People's Innovation Company. An inspiration fee is charged for inventions that resemble existing IP rights, which is paid to the owner of the IP right in question. Many inventors can use the patent camera to document their collaboration and track who contributed how much to the invention, or simply document their invention for filing.

The **Ideas Directory** takes the form of a digital platform where inventors can obtain a profile to search for similar inventions, file for a suitable IP right and compete for funding, collaborators, producers and customers. Inventors can form joint inventor groups across the country. The most pressing unsatisfied needs of the population can be found in the digital challenge search engine on the basis of polls.

For **Innovation promotion**, companies and inventors who are a good match are networked to commercialise an invention under licence, under contract or by themselves. **Innovation news** for companies contain new inventions which are useful to these companies. For inventors, they contain relevant companies and similar new inventions. For researchers, they contain the latest research results in their field.

Innovation workshops can be used in the Social Villages in order to produce prototypes and small series. The costs only have to be paid off afterwards in the form of profit-sharing. Inventors can arrange for the Ministry of Media Affairs to produce a promotional video, which is broadcast once free of charge on state-run News Television and can be screened in shops so that consumers can order the invention. All domestically registered inventions are exhibited at trade fairs, world exhibitions and in the Museum of Innovation.

The **Innovation Database** allows companies to document their trade secrets, proprietary and nascent innovations and share them with other paying companies through the innovation auditors. This is a private section of the Ideas Directory not accessible to the public. Volunteers can share their ideas with companies and ministries in the **Innovation meetings**. If an idea is implemented, the inventor is rewarded. If the idea already existed at the company or as a property right, the innovation auditors prove this using the Innovation Database and Ideas Directory. The Company Auditing Agency identifies innovative employees via questionnaires and invites them to the Innovation Congress, where other companies canvass for them. **Cartels for innovation** are approved by the Antitrust Agency for a maximum of 20 years. In an Innovation Community, companies are allowed to agree on price agreements, purchasing cooperations, non-compete agreements, market divisions, exclusive purchasing or supply obligations, which the Antitrust Agency examines and approves or demands changes. Environmental innovations are paid for by levying a price surcharge on environmentally harmful products that they will replace. The **Ideas Stock Exchange** exists for financing other innovations, where innovation bonds, innovation shares, licence participation shares and product shares can be traded. The **Innovation Fund** also provides seed money for all inventors and obliges successful inventors who once received money from this fund to pay in 5 per cent of their annual profits every year. Companies that hinder innovation provoke a procrastination of innovation and are punished.

People's Innovation Companies are formed as soon as an IP right is filed that shows global promise and is accepted by the People's Innovation Company Commission. Prior to publication, inventors are asked whether they want to market their invention through a People's Innovation Company. Company Auditing Agency auditors and business consultants take over the planning and foundation. The Construction Team takes over the construction work following successful consultation with local residents. Costs for construction and equipment are borne by the People's Innovation Company fund, into which existing People's Innovation Companies pay and income from People's Innovation Company product shares flows. Corporate governance corresponds to that of a joint-stock company in the Social Market Economy. Prior to privatisation, 15% of the shares are allotted to inventors, 15% to employees and 70% to the Ministry of Innovation. Directors are elected directly by the shareholders. The people can also be granted voting rights through the veto quorum. The People's Innovation Company can issue product shares for the production of ordered products, i.e. take out loans on the Ideas Stock Exchange, which are repaid as soon as the product is sold. The People's Innovation Company can issue product shares for expensive products, which shareholders buy so that they can rent out the product. People's Innovation Companies establish industrial communities with suitable domestic companies, which then pay only 50% business tax. People's Innovation Companies make monopoly profits on their unique and proprietary products. 15 per cent of the profits go to the inventors, 10 per cent to People's Innovation Company research and development, 10 per cent to the Research Cost Fund, 14 per cent as bonuses on top of wages for employees, 1 per cent to the People's Innovation Company Fund and the remaining 50 per cent to the national treasury. VAT decreases accordingly. If a People's Innovation Company makes losses for 3 years in a row, it is shut down. After the IPR expires, the People's Innovation Company is privatised by selling the shares owned by the Ministry of Innovation on the People's Stock Exchange.

The **People's Innovation Company Think Tank** cannot be privatised or closed down, because its mission is the ongoing development and commercialisation of inventions. As soon as at least 5 people can be found who want to develop ideas together, they establish a think tank. As soon as the size of the group reaches 10 people, another group is formed. Each group works through its members' ideas in turn and exchanges ideas with specialists from other groups throughout the country. Think tanks use appropriate government premises for their meetings or set up an inventors' group in the Ideas Directory. The People's Innovation Company Think Tank procures materials for its groups and runs the innovation workshops. It arranges cooperations with domestic companies and the Innovation Agency. The People's Innovation Company Think Tank is financed by a 1 per cent share of the annual profit that entrepreneurs transfer to or licensees who have developed the idea in a think tank.

The **People's Innovation Company 3D printer halls** construct and operate halls where any product up to the size of a building can be built. Various print heads and milling machines travel through the hall on cranes and trolleys.

The Ministry of Innovation pursues **Symbol policy** by declaring a Day of Good Ideas, holding prize competitions and contests, building statues for great native inventors, and running a Museum of Innovation with all nationally registered inventions.

Chapter 13: Education

The Ministry of Education pursues an education policy that provides an engaging, understandable and easily accessible education for the whole population. It undertakes the education and training of staff for the civil service and childcare for all state employees. Its language department handles the translation of conversations or texts for all ministries.

The **Education system** is designed to be democratically governed and to accord educational institutions autonomy in the spirit of subsidiarity. Central guidelines enable the uniform entry, transfer and completion of programmes at educational institutions throughout the country. The demand on the labour market for the relevant qualifications is announced in advance at the beginning and before the final examination. Learning goals assure a uniform minimum level of skills are entailed by a particular educational qualification.

This involves having an adequate knowledge of people and the environment in order to be able to control oneself. That in turn means researching and developing of one's own learning behaviour and the appropriate teaching method. This is covered by training based on a curriculum that qualifies one for certain professions.

The **Institute for Education** constantly seeks out and researches suitable educational institutions and companies, degrees and professions, as well as teaching methods and learning types. It evaluates surveys conducted among students. The curriculum is democratically drawn up at a public meeting with the Ministers of Education, Labour and Innovation and representatives from authorities, business associations and educational institutions to determine current and future occupational requirements. The people can lodge an appeal and voice their opinion. Together with the teachers, the students determine the implementation of the requirements from the curriculum in their educational institution in a democratic process. Financing is largely provided by school-age children, whose education and all-day care, including during holiday supervision, is paid for through child benefit. In addition, the educational institutions themselves generate income with education through work and research. The rest is made up of tax funds.

According to the principle of **Education through work**, students perform compulsory services both within their educational institution and outside it in cooperation with neighbouring educational institutions and companies. Students and teachers regularly visit and support each other through educational mentorships between nursery school and primary school, primary school and comprehensive school, comprehensive school and college. Learners take responsibility for younger students, supervising them, helping them with their homework and tutoring them. This cooperation helps to reduce costs for teachers. Students receive classroom visits from employees at companies, perform some production and research work for companies in class, and visit neighbouring companies as part of their classes, work placements and vocational training. Production and research for companies generate income for the educational institutions, replacing taxpayers' money.

According to the principle of **Education through research**, the contents of the curriculum are explored in everyday situations and researched through textbooks and experiments rather than learnt. This ensures that doctrinal opinions continue to be accessed and questioned. Learning activities of this kind often generate ideas by which improvements and inventions can be made. Learners keep ideas diaries and can rely on their course supporting them as they explore and develop their idea. If an idea is ground-breaking, the entire educational institution or all educational institutions in the entire country can be brought together in a research alliance until the idea can be commercialised. This collaboration generates revenue from royalties, which flow proportionately to the educational institutions.

Teachers are trained according to standardised requirements, paid according to performance and dismissed if their performance is poor. Surveys of students and the results of their centralised performance records provide the requisite data. Their careers include completing 10 years of work experience in authorities and companies similar to their profession, on an hourly, weekly or monthly basis, in between their teaching duties. The correction of the anonymised performance records and examinations is never carried out by the student's teacher, but by an external teacher or a computer programme and, on a random basis, by the Examinations Office.

The individual **Educational institutions** take the form of special schools, nursery schools, primary schools, comprehensive schools, colleges, vocational training colleges, universities and adult education centres. Special day-care centres and primary schools in Social Villages also care for the children of incapacitated parents around the clock, every day of the week. The education system is digitalised so that all files relating to students are kept digitally in the **Education Directory** and are seamlessly transferred between educational institutions. Students are also given the opportunity to create their own timetable, form groups and rate and comment on content. Teachers have the opportunity to design their own duty roster and plan their lessons across subjects. Democratic governance is achieved through quorums, student councils and committees, parents', teachers' and administrators' councils and educational tribunals. Education courts are courts of arbitration conducted by students, teachers and, where appropriate, parents to settle disputes.

The **Rights of learners** include, in addition to the democratic representation of their interests, a duty to provide information and a system of counselling and complaints via the Education Authority. Minors are required to attend primary and comprehensive school between the ages of 6 and 18. All adult nationals are free to attend all educational institutions throughout their lives to catch up on qualifications. The Knowledge Directory and digital teaching methods are available to all the people in the world, making the distance learning of all national qualifications possible. Prior knowledge is examined and documented certificates of achievement are accepted. Direct registration for a final examination is possible at any time.

Education tests on developmental levels, learning types and intelligence enable students and teachers to adapt to each other. Depending on the learning type, students can choose between frontal teaching, project teaching or free learning, as well as between a written, oral or project-based examination.

The Examinations Office produces the same central **Performance records** and final examinations for all educational institutions in the country. The only marks that count towards passing a course or completing an educational pathway are the assessments from the central performance records or final examinations. Following performance assessments, those students who have done well explain how they studied and clarify any outstanding questions. Teachers are expected to learn from this how to explain things in a more comprehensible way and share successful learning methods with all teachers in the education system. Educational institutions also teach and assess learners' **Work and social behaviour** to teach them a sense of precision, physical control and duty, as well as a willingness to learn, a feeling for hierarchy and the ability to work in a team. When bullying occurs, there is a regulated procedure for punishment and psychological reappraisal.

Punitive measures are non-violent in all educational institutions and are taken when someone deliberately disrupts lessons or hinders others in their learning, including breaks. These are limited to punitive work, detention, parental conferences, fines, expulsion and upbringing camps. The legal process for severe punishments and challenges to punishments begins in the education court.

Special schools exist for the behaviourally disturbed, those with learning difficulties and the highly gifted. They are situated in the Social Villages.

Nursery school educates and cares for children from the age of 2 until they start school. The children can choose for themselves whether they want to be in a static group or in varying thematic rooms. The central performance records and final examinations are carried out by playing games and through observation methods, which at the same time identify the children's interests and talents, and on which teachers then base their learning programmes. Primary school teachers take over the pre-school work in the nursery school.

Primary school is shaped by classes and school years. The timetables and teachers are set for the students. They can determine the seating arrangement, teaching method, projects and change of school entirely or partially on their own. The subjects taught include the official language of the country, maths, writing and design, ethics, sex education, People's Computer, art, physical education, music, local and general studies, textile work and manual crafts. For their 10th birthday, primary school pupils receive their People's Computer as a gift and the right to vote for the Ministries of Education and Family. Afternoon care is not part of compulsory education and follows the same care approach as for a day-care centre. Staff from the day-care centre look after the primary school pupils in the afternoon and are supported by volunteer senior citizens and clubs.

Comprehensive school is shaped by courses, certificates and weekly hours. Students can choose the degree they want to study and accordingly have to acquire certain certificates. Certificates are awarded in courses on specific subjects from the curriculum. Teachers offer courses and students enrol in these courses to create their timetable. When choosing a course, students also choose their teacher, the type of examination and the method and type of teaching. The course description already states whether a written, oral or project-based examination is offered, whether frontal teaching, project teaching or free learning is offered and whether the lessons take place weekly or as a block course. Certificates can be repeated up to four times, after which they can be repeated as often as desired in the special school. School subjects are offered for one year only or for six years. Accordingly, they are completed with one certificate or six certificates. Single-year subjects include learning, inventing, voting, integration, nutrition, applying for a job and building a house. Multi-year subjects include the official language of the country, maths, physical education, economics, music, computer science, chemistry, physics, biology, geography, technology, manual crafts, politics, history, psychology, ethics, foreign languages and art. The foreign languages taught are English, Spanish, French, Russian and Chinese. A minimum number must be selected from the multi-year subjects. 20 hours per week is the minimum number of hours required for compulsory education. The students look after each other by providing tutoring, leisure activities and services for the canteen. During international exchanges, comprehensive school students learn their set foreign language and, during student exchanges, get to know a different way of life in their region. The final years 11 to 13 are shaped by the final examinations and in-depth studies. They consist of the basic qualification after 11 years of learning, the advanced qualification after 12 years of learning and the college entrance qualification after 13 years of learning. At the end of compulsory schooling, pupils can also leave the comprehensive school without a school-leaving certificate. Their schooling stay can also be extended at will until the desired qualification is achieved if they are able to support themselves or move into the Social Village.

Comprehensive school is followed by the **People's Service**, where persons have to work for the state or non-profit organisations for one year at the minimum wage in the Social Market Economy. 3 months of basic military training in country defence and in the People's Protection Service are compulsory. The services in the remaining 9 months can be chosen freely.

Colleges are made up of vocational training colleges, scientific training and free research colleges, and state research universities. They offer study in various subject areas, but only a university is obliged to offer all subject areas. One has to apply to colleges and go through an acclimatisation period. As soon as a certificate average limits admission, the missing capacities are made up, provided there is sufficient demand in the labour market. A performance record is required for performance certificates, while attending a course is sufficient for attendance certificates. Otherwise, teaching is predominantly the same as at a comprehensive school. Students are responsible for cleaning and catering at the university. The university degree determines the course of study pursued and consist of Bachelor's degree, Master's Craftsperson degree, Diploma degree and Master's Graduate degree. Students, teachers and researchers are involved in research and assist one another. Research undertaken at colleges serves research communities consisting of several colleges nationwide or worldwide, government institutes, policy advisors and corporate research projects. Central performance records and final theses may be commissioned accordingly.

The **Free education** system allows anyone to acquire knowledge and earn degrees at any time. Whereas educational institutions and boarding schools in the Social Village are only open to nationals, adult education centres and digitalised, passive or global education offerings are accessible to all. Digitalised education facilitates interactive distance learning through the collaboration between educational institutions, Educational Television and the People's Innovation Company Intranet. Those who pass all digital examinations can take the relevant final examination at the appropriate educational institution directly.

The **Knowledge Directory** stores and publishes all learning materials free of charge on the intranet and Internet. It also offers an automated assessment of the user's prior knowledge and checks and corrects examination results. The educational content for all educational institutions is digitised on an ongoing basis, in that students can also submit their performance records as videos or computer programmes. Educational Television provides for continuous filming, and the Knowledge Directory provides for extensive storage.

Chapter 14: Health

The Ministry of Health is tasked with creating a healthy environment for people, animals and plants and empowering them to cure themselves of diseases and poisoning. It provides for operational health management in all state institutions, takes care of the treatment, education and prevention of workplace accidents, controls and provides health and safety at work.

The **Healthcare system** is structured into a network in which quality assurance and research are continuously undertaken. Institutes of the Ministry of Health are responsible for the measurement, research and development of test methods, limit values, protective measures and innovations. The health authorities and the health inspectors from the Company Auditing Agency are responsible for their implementation. The Minister of Health calls the people to attend a health committee whenever ethical or fundamental rights issues arise in health policy. Health disasters that affect the majority of the population are considered extraordinary situations. The Minister of Health then has more state powers, coordinating and exercising them with the people prior to the occurrence of an extraordinary situation.

In the context of **Health care**, patients are free to choose which doctors they want to be treated by, and to compare the diagnosis and treatment methods of several doctors. However, they can only choose a cure from one doctor at the expense of the health insurance. Another treatment method can only be used if this does not lead to recovery. All medical treatments and measures are recorded, compiled, evaluated and improved in the Health Directory. Citizens receive a **Health Card** for data collection and treating physicians are afforded insight into all the patient's medical data ever compiled.

Physicians are licensed by the Health Department and initially and regularly audited by health inspectors. Doctors are medical practitioners who practise conventional medicine and healers who practise alternative healing methods. They specialise in a medical field or in paediatric medicine, veterinary medicine and herbal medicine and are organised in the Medical Association. The **Medical Fee Schedule** is negotiated between the Medical Association, the Minister of Health and the health insurance providers. It regulates the payment of staff, equipment and buildings by law, although Free Market Economy companies are not bound by these regulations. The digital health system identifies, communicates and researches particularly gentle and curative treatments. The Ministry of Health runs government health centres in Social Villages, which are a mixture of hospital and doctors' surgery. It conducts research and development in its university hospitals in collaboration with its institutes and the Ministry of Education.

Care is provided differently in the different economic forms. The individual models differ in various respects, for example with regard to paid services provided by professionals to mutual family or neighbourhood organised care. The need for care is determined in care levels. The Care Directory allows those in need of care, and professional, family and honorary carers to find each other, as well as to form residential and care communities.

Medicines are prescribed by doctors, matched to the patient by pharmacists and manufactured by the **Pharmaceutical industry**. The pharmaceutical industry in the Barter Economy and Planned Economy is more oriented towards medicinal plants, while the pharmaceutical industry in the Social Market Economy and Free Market Economy is more oriented towards chemical products. The digital health system constantly identifies, researches and remedies side effects and interactions.

Drugs are dispensed in pharmacies to educate users at the time of first purchase and to warn of side effects with diseases, medicines or other **Drugs**. The Health Card is then augmented to become a drug card and records consumption, even if it is in a restaurant. The pharmaceutical industry is responsible for the production of drugs and researches intoxicants with the same effect but fewer health risks. A purity law applies to the production of all drugs.

There are only three **Health insurance companies** in order to keep the level of bureaucracy as low as possible. All other health insurance types take the form of supplementary insurance for extra services that can be accessed in the Free Market Economy. General Health Insurance covers all legal owed benefits under the Medical Fee Schedule if they are caused by accidents, illnesses or damages. Contributions and benefits are decided upon democratically by the insured parties. Services required due to the consumption of addictive substances are not covered. The Addictive Drugs Health Insurance exists for this purpose. Its contributions come from price surcharges on addictive substances. Neither does general health insurance cover benefits to be provided above the age of 80 or 3 months before the expected date of death in the case of a fatal disease. The Immortality Health Insurance exists for this purpose. It is the task of the Ministry of Health to establish legal requirements for medical research, **Reproduction** and **Transplantation**. Research involving human beings has to be consented to by the person concerned. Animal experiments are not allowed to torture the animal, but it must be treated according to its species. Abortions, artificial insemination, sperm donation, surrogate motherhood and genetic testing are permitted for the purpose of free procreation. Children, on the other hand, have the right to know who their biological parents are. Organ donors can be any dying person who does not object and who has the information recorded on their Health Card. Artificial organs can be freely traded, but must not be allowed to grow in a body with a consciousness.

Health prevention consists mainly of recommendations and guidelines issued by the Ministry of Health. Thanks to the digital health system, citizens receive personalised recommendations from their physicians and in their profile in the Health Directory on how to eat healthily and exercise sufficiently. Companies and ministries are issued guidelines by the institutes within the Ministry of Health regarding when food and products are safe for health, biodegradable, recyclable or dangerous.

The **Sustainable use of nature** means that future generations will also be able to rely on the same biodiversity in stable ecosystems. Endangered species are protected in wildlife sanctuaries. Specifications for animal and plant protection prevent the contamination of food and soil with fertilisers, poisons, medicines and stress hormones. In cooperation with the Ministries of Labour, Infrastructure and Innovation, specifications are made and measures planned that concern marine protection, agriculture and genetic engineering.

Environmental protection is achieved with the cooperation of the population, guidelines for companies and measures taken by other ministries. Citizens and authorities report environmental pollution to the Environment Directory, where they also work together to organise its clean-up. Guidelines for companies provide for a maximum burden on the environment that does not exceed the natural capacity for regeneration. Waste has to be either biodegradable, reusable or harmlessly storable. Goods that do not guarantee such environmentally neutral disposal are prohibited or not allowed in the first place. Persons or companies that pollute the environment are investigated by the police or health inspectors and brought to justice. Polluters are required to repair the damage they have caused and are imprisoned for as long as it would take nature to clean up the pollution without human intervention. In cleaning up environmental disasters, entire industries can be held liable to pay the follow-up costs.

Structural change is part of healthcare and becomes necessary when a way of life has become a global health hazard. Global warming causes **Climate change**, the consequences of which are mitigated and causes reversed. The Ministry of Health sets targets and implements measures together with the Ministries of Labour and Infrastructure. Reefs made of shells protect the coasts, water reservoirs and new construction methods protect against natural disasters. Permaculture binds water and carbon dioxide, filters toxins from water, air and soil and multiplies the amount of food available at lower prices. Renewable energy provides electricity and heat from biomass, sun, wind, water, waves and tides and requires no regular use of additional raw materials. Surplus energy is stored in pumped-storage power stations, hydrogen, salt, methane or compressed air. The efficiency of generation and consumption is doubled. Finite raw materials force a structural change through which they no longer need to be mined because they are replaced by renewable alternatives and reused or recycled in a circular economy. Switching to **Bioeconomy** means that all goods in demand grow from a biodegradable nutrient solution by means of genetically controlled cell growth. Supply chains become shorter, raw materials are almost infinitely available thanks to the oceans, disposal costs are almost completely eliminated. The aim of every structural change is to use new technologies to save so much in costs that their cost of purchase quickly pays for itself, so that they can then finance the clean-up of contaminated sites.

Chapter 15: Infrastructure

The Ministry of Infrastructure is tasked with providing the majority of the country's inhabitants with the home they want, with environmentally friendly and fast mobility, with a home ownership rate of over 90 per cent and with an independent energy supply from renewable energy sources. It provides housing for all state employees.

The Ministry of Infrastructure pursues **Homeland** security, by means of which the country's territory is built on in a targeted and controlled manner or remains undeveloped. The aim is to ensure that all citizens or local residents agree and that the environment is not polluted. The same applies to the extraction of **Raw materials** which also uses resulting overburdens and fills in excavations. The extraction of finite raw materials is replaced by renewable substitutes or a circular economy. The Institute for Geosciences and Natural Resources develops and combines such methods and surveys the land with a view to approving construction and quarrying projects. State green spaces are planted with edible plants whose fruits and foliage are available free of charge to citizens, farmers and biogas plants. **Urban development** takes place in consultation with residents, and the establishment and expansion of cities is coordinated with the people or surrounding municipalities. Individuals and cooperatives can purchase housing on a rent-to-own scheme which has been created through the housebuilding programme until the home ownership rate reaches 90 per cent. Foreigners are not allowed to buy or own land inside the country. The real estate market is digitalised in the **Real Estate Directory** so that land and buildings can be found, bought and rented there, and housing communities can be formed to build, buy or rent.

The Ministry of Infrastructure provides open workshops, covered areas, recreational areas, bathing lakes, barbecue areas, trim trails and public restaurants so that citizens can enjoy their leisure time in public spaces. It also authorises a street festival once a year for each street. The **State Utilities** operate the national grids and power stations for energy supply, as well as the weather service and Alliance of Municipal Utilities. The **Municipal Utilities Companies** provide data, electricity, heat, water and the disposal of liquids, solids and gases. They partner with citizens who generate and share sufficient electricity and heat within the municipality with their buildings. They supply biogas from biogas plants, heat from zeolite, liquid salt or computing power from computers as heating or in the form of hot water boilers, and hydrogen from solar cell electrolysis, which can be used to store or generate heat or electricity.

The **Water supply** with clean drinking water and the treatment of wastewater is the task of the Municipal Utilities Companies, which share water in the network of State Utilities in the event of water shortages and separate industrial water and drinking water in different circuits. Drinking water sources are not allowed to belong to foreigners and in case of an imminent water shortage, domestic companies can be prohibited from pumping it.

Waste disposal is taken care of by the Municipal Utilities Companies via collection and recycling plants. Generally, producers have to pay for the disposal of their products and coordinate their production with the disposal companies so that recycling is guaranteed. The disposal companies set the costs for disposal, and the producers have to add these costs to their sale price and pay them to the disposal companies. Waste disposal is therefore always free for citizens and public waste bins are widely available. Citizens promote the circular economy through their bulk waste, which is deposited on the street as public property, collected 2 days later by social services and the rest thereafter by waste collection service. Rubbish disposed of in the natural environment is collected by citizen volunteers, and primary and comprehensive school pupils.

The **Building**, management and maintenance of all state buildings is undertaken by the local Building Yard, sometimes in cooperation with the Construction Team. Citizens can vote collectively on building projects, which are built in cooperation with the Building Yard. The Building Department checks and approves building projects for their safety for people and the environment. Relevant specifications for buildings include load-bearing statics, even in the event of floods, storms and earthquakes, the recyclability of building materials, and buildings that generate more energy than they consume. Loans for energy-efficient construction make it possible to keep the costs for consumers the same, thereby paying off the loan and having no more costs for energy afterwards. Specifications for cities, grids and transport routes include environmentally friendly and energy-generating road surfaces, streetlamps equipped with solar cells, and consultations with citizens concerning renovations or extensions. All construction projects are profiled in the **Infrastructure Directory** so that citizens can create virtual construction plans, discuss them with one another on the noticeboard, unite to form building groups and participate in the construction. The Materials Database can be used to order building materials and furnishings for a price and borrow construction machinery and tools that are state-owned.

The **Construction Team** is organised militarily, uses all personnel and materials from the Building Yards and builds structures in the shortest possible time at any location in the country. It uses huge construction machines, referred to as **Infrastructureators**, which are manufactured by People's Innovation Companies, and houses its many construction workers in living containers at the construction site. The Construction Team is made up of full-time professionals, teachers and students of the appropriate subject from the educational institutions, volunteers, People's Service providers and prisoners. The Ministry of Infrastructure operates **Mobile cities** with container modules for housing and all necessary trades for supply. Mobile towns are used during major construction projects or disasters. They otherwise serve in whole or in part as a mobile prison or Social Village.

The task of the **Housebuilding programme** is to have the Construction Team build housing estates and neighbourhoods. The sites are located where there is a housing shortage, many high-rise buildings exist, a sufficient number of citizens have voted for it in the Real Estate Directory and surrounding municipalities agree with the building project. The housebuilding programme is financed on credit, which is paid off through the rent-to-own scheme for all new owners. Students and future owners work on the construction sites. At least 20 per cent of the new owners must be from the same locality. Once 90 per cent of all nationals live in their own homes, the housebuilding programme is terminated.

The Ministry of Infrastructure builds and operates **Networks** for pedestrians, vehicles, trains, ships, aircraft, electricity, data, drinking water, sewage, salt water, waste and liquid or gaseous fuels. The networks for raw materials and goods transport are located in an underground tunnel. It forms a grid structure underground, connects the coasts with the mountains, uses the natural gradient for pumped-storage power stations along the route and converts waste heat from the pipelines into electricity in heat exchangers.

The **Traffic** networks for people are digital in the air and magnetic levitation trains and local roads on land. Flying cars for long-distance travel move in autopilot through digital corridors in the sky at different altitudes and in different directions. They only use the roads from the landing site to the final destination. Goods are transported from unloading stations by truck up to 4 metric tons in total weight over the roads to their final destination. A toll is charged for using the roads for all vehicles with a total weight of 100 kilos or more. Existing trunk roads are to be demolished or converted into cycle paths as soon as magnetic levitation trains and flying cars are introduced. Until then, a minimum speed of 130 km/h will apply on motorways and a maximum speed of 200 km/h for digitally networked vehicle convoys. Intercontinental travel will take place from spaceports with spaceships that do not cause space debris. The Ministry of Infrastructure arranges for the collection of space debris and charges the costs to the originators that cause the pollution. Magnetic levitation trains allow for long-distance and continental travel, as well as the transfer with exit carriages during the journey. They run on columns under which vehicles can pass. Local public transport runs on tracks above and below ground. Waterways are used for shipping, recreation and groundwater level control. Anglers, water sports enthusiasts and sailors are not allowed to use items that can pollute the waters and are not naturally biodegradable. Ships convert their propulsion systems to electricity and hydrogen or are no longer allowed to call at inland ports. Flood basins along river courses prevent flooding, serve as water reservoirs and pumped-storage power stations. All means of transport are powered by electricity or hydrogen and it must be possible to replace all batteries quickly at filling stations. The Department of Transport monitors traffic safety and environmental protection requirements in cooperation with Company Auditing Agency auditors. The Transport Directory makes it possible for citizens to view all public transport timetables, book tickets and join carpools.

The supply of **Energy** is guaranteed by the infinite and free power of the moon, water, sun and Earth's gravity, as well as by the difference in temperature between the earth, air and water. Regulations for engines and power plants increase efficiency. Insulation and innovations reduce energy consumption. The energy transition is mutually funded. Any gains from old energy sources are used to build new energy sources. The profits from the new energy sources pay for the disposal costs for the old energy sources. The costs to consumers meanwhile remain the same and thereafter fall to the maintenance costs of the new energy sources. In the Energy Directory, State Utilities, Municipal Utilities, private producers and consumers trade in electricity and heat. There, groups are formed that can provide themselves with sufficient energy. The energy supply is guaranteed nationally and locally.

The State Utilities produce **Centralised** electricity with wind farms, current, wave and tidal power plants off the coast and transport it through the country through tunnels. They also pump water from the coasts to the mountains to underground flood basins and reservoirs. There they store excess electricity or use it for electrolysis and generate hydrogen. Filter systems between the marine power plants filter plastic waste from the water. On land, they operate solar, sail and wind power plants at suitable locations. Vertically rotating wind power plants are installed in the middle of power poles.

The municipal utilities operate biogas plants, run-of-river power plants, pumped storage power plants and self-sufficient government buildings in a **Decentralised** manner. Citizens operate self-sufficient buildings which, depending on their size and energy consumption, also supply electricity and gas. They have roof tiles that generate electricity and heat from the sun, as well as barred, vertically rotating wind turbines on the roof. Zeolite modules on the facade dry there in summer and give off heat in winter in the central heating system through water supply. Rainwater from the roof is channelled between floors through an in-house pumped storage power plant, providing power and cooling. It is fed into a water tank in the floor, which runs a heat exchanger. Electrolysis is operated with this water and excess electricity. The hydrogen can be sold over the gas pipeline or stored in a tank and converted back into electricity by a fuel cell or into heat in a furnace.

Municipal Utilities Companies offer combined orders and installation on credit. The loan is paid off by paying the usual energy prices and additional feeds into the grid. After that, the energy costs for the building drop to the maintenance costs for the installations. This means that energy can become free within 25 years. New sources of electricity are being developed in the Tesla lab and lightning power stations are being tested. Future energy sources include biotechnological processes, for example the transplantation of chloroplasts into muscle cells or the generation of adenosine triphosphate in nutrient solutions.

Chapter 16: Security

The Ministry of Security is tasked with protecting the people of the country and guarding the democratic state in which they live. Through the police, the ministry provides protection against sabotage in all ministries.

The Security Minister is responsible for national and international **Security policy** and their deputy in the municipality is responsible for municipal security policy. At municipal level, security forces can be more lenient or stricter and enforce municipal laws if a majority of the citizens in the municipality are in favour.

The **Security forces** assist one another. They are allowed to restrict the fundamental right to liberty when they cordon off accident or crime scenes, issue expulsions and house bans or carry out arrests and detentions. They may violate the fundamental right to bodily integrity if they are insulted, assaulted or obstructed in the course of their duties. Only nationals are allowed to be employed by the Ministry of Security. All persons are obliged to provide first aid and make provisional arrests if imminent danger exists and they are not putting themselves in danger by doing so. In emergencies of this kind, they should always call in the security forces as well. Foreigners may serve in the fire brigade, rescue service and Technical Relief Agency. Private security services are prohibited and are replaced by the People's Protection Service. The monopoly of force is composed of the police, the People's Protection Service, customs and the military and has to be state and democratically controlled. Security forces have a duty to wear their badge number or name visibly and to announce the legal basis for their action, unless they are working undercover. Victims can file complaints against the security forces with the Public Prosecutor's Office. Security forces are provided with versatile walkie-talkies by the People's Innovation Company Intranet. During security operations they use blue lights and sirens, during social and disaster relief operations they use green lights and music.

The **Security Directory** represents a combination of the operational command, administration and citizen oversight. Security organs are given a profile, security forces organise themselves into groups and store their work files there. Sub-groups can be opened for a case and then closed again. Investigative tactical and personal data is anonymised for public viewing, but can be used in court if charges are brought against the security forces. In the event of a disaster, all citizens are assigned to services over the Security Directory.

Weapons law allows police and the People's Protection Service to use non-lethal close combat weapons, at an early stage, such as batons or pepper spray, and long-range weapons, such as stun guns, rubber bullets, poison dart launchers, net launchers or drones equipped with non-lethal close combat and long-range weapons. Special operations units and the military are allowed to use lethal weapons. Private individuals such as hunters and members of shooting clubs are allowed to own and use lethal weapons, but they need a firearms licence and have to buy and store the weapons at the local police station. Lethal weapons and weapons of war are only allowed to be manufactured in state Planned Enterprises to meet domestic demand. All suitable companies convert their production to serve the war economy if the situation requires. The import and export of lethal weapons is prohibited.

Commercial organisers of **Large events** must hire and pay for security guards. If their customers cause disturbances outside the event, this also has to be paid for or the organiser will be banned from the profession. **Demonstrations** are to be announced in advance if possible. If the demonstration is attended by more than 100 people, the police have to be informed in order to guarantee the traffic safety during the procession. Peaceful demonstrators are to immediately report violent demonstrators to the police or arrest them provisionally. Violent demonstrations will be stopped and must be followed up by a demo TV show, in which causes and solutions are identified.

In a **State of emergency**, security forces are required to abide by the law and, in the event of a coup d'état, to join with citizens to form communal vigilante groups. **Terrorism** is combated by not engaging in foreign hostilities, exploitation or claims to power and by democratically integrating political minorities at home via committees, municipal laws and cultural protection areas. **Social hotspots** where many criminals live are broken up. Residents are resettled in Social Villages or participate in the housebuilding programme. **Memorials** are set up at places where the events took place in order to be able to understand the acts and avoid them in the future. Memorials at neutral sites will be phased out.

For the **Prevention of danger** there will be full-time and voluntary civil defence bodies deployed in all municipalities. If a sufficient number of private companies or volunteers cannot be found, the Ministry of Security will run these civil defence bodies. Honorary civil defence officers practice in their free time and are released from work and compensated for operations. If a disaster occurs, civil defence bodies are called together nationwide. Civil defence is composed of the rescue services, fire brigade and Technical Relief Agency. State **Rescue service**s are always on-site in health centres and university hospitals. Rescue services travel to the nearest free hospital. The **Fire brigade** tackles accidents with fire, earth, water and air. Extinguishing water is fired at the sources of the fire using compressed air cannons. As a preventive measure, the water rescue service protects the public in bodies of water. The **Technical Relief Agency** furnishes the necessary pumps, water treatment plants, power generators, lighting equipment, excavators, cranes mobile supply buildings and dwellings during large-scale operations. The equipment can also be used in the event of war and is therefore painted in camouflage colours.

The **People's Work Service** take precautionary measures against natural disasters, for example by erecting dams, and practising their services to prepare for various catastrophes. Citizens of full age can be obligated in this service if not enough volunteers can be found.

All security forces can always be contacted using the **Emergency number 110**. Over the intranet and Internet, emergency calls can be made on the police website, from abroad using the country code and 110, or in person at any police station. Moreover, each ID card has a one-time emergency feature that makes an emergency call by snapping off and pulling out a corner and sends a localisation signal. If a social intervention occurs, the People's Protection Service is notified and assisted by the social service.

The Minister of Security is responsible for national **Disaster management** and their deputies for protection within their municipalities. Risk analyses and emergency plans are prepared for all catastrophic events such as war, trade restrictions, economic failures, crimes, accidents, fires, floods, droughts, storms, earthquakes, volcanic eruptions, tsunamis, pandemics, meteorite impacts, solar storms and pole reversals. Emergency plans are drawn up together with the population in committees, coordinated and regularly drilled. Every citizen is assigned to a service that they carry out in the event of a catastrophe. Victims know what will happen to them and when normality will return. All citizens and businesses can be called upon to serve in the event of a catastrophe and receive appropriate compensation. Emergency alarm signals in the form of sirens on town hall rooftops inform the population of the rehearsed emergency scenario. Catastrophe protection starts with training and exercises, saves lives during the emergency and, if necessary, evacuates the population impacted. The operation does not end until the reconstruction is completed. To aid reconstruction, civil defence sets up shuttle services that bring helpers and craftspersons to the area of the disaster and provides them with accommodation and food. The equipment is designed to be used outside a catastrophic event as well. If the equipment is not needed at home, it can be used to provide paid **International disaster management** by housing the population affected and for evacuation, education and reconstruction measures.

The **People's Protection Service** provides stand-by services for all other security organs and the social service. This takes the form of a security service that companies can hire and provides defence troops when citizens call for them in a quorum. Its personnel consist of non-defence soldiers, as well as citizen volunteers and People's Service providers. Their equipment is military but no arms, and includes non-lethal weapons, body armour, helmets, walkie-talkies, gloves, rubbish bags, cable ties, multi-functional tools, and a body injury billing device including a wallet. A police officer carries out patrol duty together with a protection squad from the People's Protection Service. The patrol is tasked with settling disputes, if required in mediation cells, and facilitating duels and fights in secured zones for those who are willing to use violence, and billing for bodily injuries on-site so that the injuries of opponents do not have to be covered by the health insurance.

The **Police** are deployed to ensure internal security and work in cooperation with the Public Prosecutor's Office, the People's Protection Service and the military for this purpose. Police officers carry body cameras if they are not undercover, and non-lethal weapons if they are not attached to a special task force. The body and vehicle cameras record video that automatically flows into the digital police files in the Security Directory.

Data for pursuing prosecutions is stored in the **Investigation Directory** and sent to the Court Directory. Investigative tactical data is not visible to the public. For law enforcement purposes, police officers have access to all the data on the intranet. All searches are published in the Access Directory after the case is closed. In appropriate cases, open wanted groups for volunteer investigators are established in the Investigation Directory.

The **Civil police** investigate criminal cases in plain clothes and mostly undercover as soon as a tip-off is received. Arrests are made by uniformed police officers. In cases where criminals might have lethal weapons, trained police officers and soldiers from the People's Protection Service are equipped with lethal weapons and bulletproof vests and helmets and deploy as a special task force.

The **Digital police** investigate criminals on the Internet and intranet, handle cyber-emergency calls and are supported by military units for conducting cyber warfare. It regularly and covertly checks voting computers for attempted tampering. Cyber distress calls allow the cyber police to gain direct access to the victim's computer during or before the crime in order to secure all evidence and launch counter-attacks with obsolete military cyber weapons.

The **Institute for Criminology** researches and shares reasons for crime, organised crime, and successful methods of law enforcement, counterintelligence and anti-sabotage with investigators.

A state of emergency is declared in the event of **Riot**s. The originators are identified, grounded up in groups, numbed and arrested. Afterwards, a committee investigates the background among the population and searches for solutions.

Fighting the Mafia, their means of livelihood are withdrawn by legalising drugs and prostitution. Arms trafficking and extortion are curbed through covert investigations, abducting mafia bosses using the secret service abroad and witness protection programmes.

When the level of crime exceeds 10,000 crimes per 100,000 inhabitants, a **City raid** is conducted for a maximum of 3 days together with the military. The entire city is cordoned off, every building and person is searched, stolen goods and evidence are seized and criminals and their accomplices are arrested. Afterwards, committees are convened in the city to determine how this came about and how or if it should be prevented in the future.

The **Customs** are responsible for **Border protection** and tax investigations. At borders, automatic machines check people and goods, and customs officers check any suspicious cases. Whether the entry of foreigners is to be prohibited or restricted is reported to Customs by the Ministries of Foreign Affairs, Justice and Integration, which then enforce the directions. Foreigners with criminal convictions are not allowed to enter the country. Foreigners who want to immigrate need permission from the embassy in their country of origin. Customs perform deportations. Customs duties are levied or a ban enforced on the import or export of goods, services and capital, as specified by the Ministries of Labour, Health, Finance and Economy. Imports need a seal of approval from the Company Auditing Agency, capital is cleared at the VAT rate. Counterfeit goods, lethal weapons and goods that could introduce diseases or alien species are not allowed to be imported. Weapons are not allowed to be exported and goods from the Social Market Economy need a seal of quality prior to export. Capital is subject to a 20 per cent customs duty when exported by nationals, 60 per cent for foreigners and 40 per cent for foreign companies to compensate for the erosion of purchasing power. The **Tax Investigation Department** monitors flows of money at home and abroad, investigates tax evasion and applies for extraditions, notices to pay, entry bans and trade restrictions at the embassy in the respective foreign country. Domestically, all money flows which are not processed over the tax account are investigated and the cash cycle is monitored. Undercover investigations are carried out in case of suspected tax fraud or illicit work.

The **Military** supports the security forces and the social service with material and professional soldiers in times of peace. The remaining soldiers are all citizens who are only armed and deployed in the event of war or a coup d'état. The military can only be deployed in a foreign state that is waging a war of aggression against the homeland or its allies. Their deployment is limited to border security and the use of remotely controlled weapons. Together with allied states from the Continental Union, the military forms the Continental Defence Army and the continental Intelligence Service.

Career **Soldiers** and reservists engage in regular military exercises and all other citizens are assigned and trained once in the use of lethal weapons and operational plans for the war economy through the basic compulsory training.

During a war, the Minister of Security has to regularly consult with the people about the **Warfare**, avoid committing war crimes and surrender if necessary. In a cyber war, soldiers with suitable skills work in tandem with the cyber police and the Ministry of Digital Affairs. In a coup, the military combats coup plotters at home and conquers their territories. In a defensive war, the Continental Defence Army's external borders are defended and weapons are issued to any citizen who has already completed basic training. In a positional war, the enemy's trade shipments are seized, prisoners of war taken and the enemy's national territory attacked across the board. In an electromagnetic attack, a switch to analogue warfare takes place without the use of digital technology.

In the short term, defences will exist at the borders along with missile and laser defence shields. In the medium term, **Weapon systems** will be controlled remotely and in the long term, only weapons that can defend the earth against celestial bodies will exist. In the United States of the World, there will no longer any need for the military.

Chapter 17: Justice

The Ministry of Justice is tasked with enacting laws for procedures under the rule of law and establishing institutions such as courts and prisons where these procedures are implemented. The Ministry, together with the Public Prosecutor's Office, prosecutes disciplinary matters involving state employees. In consultation with the respective ministries, specific criminal law is enacted.

The **Principles of the rule of law** take the form of known, accessible and transparent laws, appropriate punishments in relation to the offence and impartial sentences. The **Ladder of norms** describes in descending order the law that breaks the law below it. It consists of constitutional articles, laws, court judgments, regulations, municipal laws, bylaws, administrative instructions, service instructions and habits.

All norms have profiles in the **Law Directory**, including international and continental law. Ministries, organisations, clubs or associations form groups around the norms for which they are responsible. Citizens can propose improvements by contributing posts or voting for the repeal quorum.

Areas of law divide norms into different areas. Civil law regulates disputes between citizens, criminal law regulates violations against law by citizens. State law regulates violations in which the state fails to grant citizens their rights or does so inadequately. Constitutional law applies when the state does not abide by the rules that the people have set for it.

The **Criminal law of the** 18 **ministries** serves to ensure compliance with their respective laws.

Court proceedings are heard in various courts, called instances, through what is referred to as judicial process. Court hearings are public and are stored in the Court Directory in the form of video files. Plaintiffs and defendants can be anonymised if they so wish or if they are minors. If defendants are deemed to be at risk of flight or re-offending, they are remanded in custody during the court proceedings. If the amount in dispute is less than 1,000 Dollars, or if they want to settle out of court, citizens use the digital **Arbitration Court**. In the Court Directory, lay judges pass judgement once the litigants have described the case to them and it has been simulated by the Algoracle. The legal process begins at the **Municipal Court**, which exists in every municipality. If someone does not accept the verdict because the facts were not all taken into account, they can appeal to the Remit Court. There is one **Remit Court** for each ministry, in which judges and lay judges are involved in reaching a verdict. Anyone who believes that the law has not been properly considered in full can appeal to the **National Court of Justice**. The national court also hears disputes between states, ministries and authorities. It therefore presides over itself so as not to be biased when the Ministry of Justice becomes involved in a case. It presides over the criminal component in a committee of enquiry. Judges and experienced lay judges are involved in reaching a verdict. In the verdicts, laws can be declared null and void or handed over to competent ministries for revision. If constitutional law is violated in a case, it is handed over to the **Constitutional**

Court. There, norms are examined for their compliance with the constitution. If citizens suspect a breach of the constitution, they can file a complaint before the Constitutional Court in the first instance. If norms violate the constitution, the competent ministries must amend the norms concerned within a certain period of time or enact corresponding laws. The last instance is a constitutional committee, which is convened as soon as the people consider constitutional articles to be erroneous and amend the constitution accordingly.

All court cases are assigned a profile and courts are assigned groups in the **Court Directory**. There, users can watch proceedings, evaluate judgments and vote for judges to be voted out of office in the deselection quorum. The **Court staff** consists of lawyers, patent attorneys, prosecutors, lay judges and judges. All court staff except lay judges must have a law degree with a secondary subject. This secondary subject corresponds to one of the ministries in order to be admitted to the corresponding section of the court.

Judges are elected directly. Municipal court judges are elected by the citizens in their municipality or the municipalities in the catchment area, while all other judges are elected by the people. **Lay judges** are citizens who are selected by an algorithm on the basis of their qualifications and then drawn by ballot. Judges and lay judges form a team in reaching a verdict, while the judges make the final decision. Lay judges can also participate digitally over their People's Computer.

The **Public Prosecutor's Office** represents the people in court proceedings when persons have violated laws or constitutional articles and receives complaints against security agencies. In criminal investigations, it mandates the police to conduct the necessary investigations. **Lawyers** represent plaintiffs or defendants. In the Municipal Court, plaintiffs or defendants may waive the need for a lawyer.

Court proceedings are **Financed** by the Ministry of Justice until their conclusion. The losing parties bear the costs, against which they can take out insurance with costs. Otherwise they have to pay the costs themselves and if they cannot, they have to work off the amount in prison. Proceedings in criminal and constitutional law are financed through VAT. If laws are effective and people are peaceful, the levy remains small and vice versa. Commercial proceedings and proceedings under civil and state law are paid for by the losing party. **Legal expenses insurance** is compulsory in Planned Economy and Social Market Economy, and is paid for through business tax. The Barter Economy and Free Market Economy can offer their own private legal expenses insurance policies. Lawyers are paid according to the amount in dispute and the time they spend working on the case. The Ministry of Justice sets the amounts in a table together with the Association of Lawyers. Lawyers in the Barter Economy and Free Market Economy can agree their fees contractually with their clients.

For an **Assessment of the damage**, injured parties and communities are first identified. The assessment determines the material and psychological damage they have suffered. The guideline values from insurance companies are used to determine the amounts of money to compensate the victims. If convicted persons spread fear and terror among the population with their crime, the Ministry of Justice sets additional amounts of money to compensate them. The sums of money are shown as payable in the sentence or must be worked off in whole or in part while in prison.

Clemency law make it possible to waive sentences in whole or in part. The people have the power to do this by a majority vote. Judges pardon offenders by imposing a lighter sentence, prison governors do so by furlough offenders or by transferring them to day release. Victims can waive their right to compensation with an amnesty. If the law has changed, the penalty has to be waived. Prisoners are allowed to commit suicide after 20 years at the earliest.

The various **Penal forms** are determined by the legislator and meted out by the judge on a case-by-case basis. They consist of compensation payments made by offenders to their victims. Fines are paid to the state for first-time offences where there is no violence committed against persons or property. Occupational bans are imposed on offenders who have committed a criminal offence while practising their profession. Offences without or with minor violence committed against persons or property are punished with community service at non-profit or state institutions. More serious or repeated offences are punishable by imprisonment. Judges can place minors in upbringing camps or special schools run as boarding schools instead of prisons. Sentences cannot be suspended.

While in **Detention**, the right to liberty is deprived and participation in the democratic process is restricted to voting on a voting computer. Offenders work off the harm they have caused in detention. The duration corresponds to the amount of damages divided by normal weekly working hours at the minimum wage in the Social Market Economy or is specified in the law. Prisoners are not paid wages and cannot gain access to their assets until they are freed from detention. They cannot buy or sell anything while in detention, but receive room and board. Prisons are mobile in order to be as close as possible to the place of work. They consist of container wings in the form of a cross equipped with individual cells with skylights fitted with bars and a multimedia system that communicates with the prisoner and can project peaceful worlds onto the walls of their cell. Inmates can use it to partake in virtual psychotherapy sessions and study for academic degrees. The therapy sessions are accompanied by therapists, and the degrees can be completed in an educational institution after release. Guards wear body cameras. Prisoners wear collars outside their cells which broadcast their location, monitor the ban on talking and inject sleeping pills if they try to escape. Work varies according to the inmates' previous education and potential dangerousness. Punishments for violating detention rules are limited to confinement in the cell, punitive transfer or additional menial work. Prisoners are used to perform work that is paid as much as possible above the minimum wage, so that the Ministry of Justice makes a profit rather than a loss from the prisons.

Chapter 18: Foreign Affairs

One of the tasks of the Ministry of Foreign Affairs is to attempt to remedy the negative consequences of international anarchy, imperialism and industrialisation together with voluntary states and peoples, and to reconcile the people of the world's population with one another thereafter in a federal state. It communicates to all ministries the latest information on current continental and international policies concerning the ministry in question, along with applicable international and continental law and all funding programmes starting up or in progress.

With regard to **Foreign affairs**, it maintains authorities that empower the state to act internationally. The authorities responsible for this are the Foreign Office, embassies, consulates, representations to international organisations and unions, and the Institute for Peace and Conflict Research. Any international negotiations conducted by the state have to be democratically approved by the people. The Minister of Foreign Affairs is responsible for this. The Ministry of Foreign Affairs ensures that international law and Continental Union law can be democratically rejected by the people's vote, renewed and implemented in the ministries. Together with all relevant ministries, influence is exerted on continental or international policies. Financial commitments under foreign policy are approved, scaled back or rejected by the people in the annual budget vote. Peacekeeping is a task that the Ministry of Foreign Affairs discharges by concluding peace treaties with as many states as possible.

In the long run, it is the function of the Ministry of Foreign Affairs to eliminate itself. As soon as all countries of origin are safe, development aid is concluded and the states are united, the **End of the Ministry of Foreign Affairs** is thus decided.

The aim of **Communitarisation** is to unify precepts and unite the states first throughout the continent and then throughout the world, culminating in the united states of the continent and then of the world. This task is accomplished by introducing the democratic political system of an **International Union**, which, through techniques of communitarisation, unifies precepts and increasingly and progressively unifies authorities, ministries and states. In order to set the appropriate pace, the Ministry of Foreign Affairs observes the speed at which the participating peoples integrate by voting on international treaties, supranational laws and the unification of agencies, ministries and states. In order to decouple state communitarisation from cultural integration, states with culturally similar populations are communitarised first.

The **continental policy** envisages democratising intergovernmental cooperation on one's own continent, equalising the standard of living and jointly protecting the common good of all citizens there and the territory of the continent. Democratisation follows the model of dynamic media democracy with political structures for ministries, parties and councils as well as political processes for direct elections, quorums, committees, voting, legislation and government. This entails the creation of institutions and procedures, as well as numerous changes to treaties and agreements. The country-of-destination principle applies as long as all the laws concerned are not uniform in the member states affected. If no democratic agreement is reached, the exit from the agreements follows and, if necessary, the creation of a new International Union for the continent.

International policy envisages the democratisation of the United Nations and international law, and the introduction of the international separation of powers and world peace. Areas of international policy will increasingly be uniformly regulated in order to eliminate international anarchy, exploitation, war, hunger, poverty, pollution and disease. The path to this leads through international unions on all continents to an international union for the world. This will make different speeds possible. While only minimum standards will be possible worldwide at first, states on one continent will already be so similar that they can adhere to the same laws. Each state only communitarises as fast as its population stipulates. The communitarisation process is the same worldwide so that citizens understand what is happening to them and states can unite more easily. This happens first in the culturally similar United States of the Continents and then these continental states unite to form the United States of the World. In fundamental terms, united states are federal states consisting of municipalities and nations, where the political power is given to the one who can be most effective in managing it.

Development aid is the task of the Ministry of Foreign Affairs. For this purpose it maintains the Development Agency and the Institute of Development Aid. The embassies contribute by negotiating with and providing information about the countries and regions to be developed. Development aid is only provided in one country until that country is fully developed. Only then does the next country follow. Aid starts with the least developed regions in the own country, followed by the underdeveloped neighbouring countries and then the underdeveloped neighbouring continents. Full development is considered to have been achieved when infrastructural, educational and the economic aid has provided sufficient help towards self-help. Humanitarian aid will continue to be provided within the framework of international development aid and will be made more effective in preventing death from war, famine, drought, heat and cold.

The **Asylum application procedure** is the responsibility of the Ministry of Foreign Affairs. The relevant forms are available on the Internet and the appointments are made at the embassies, which also organise travel. Embassy staff know the situation in the country in question and speak the respective language. They evaluate the safety of the countries where the asylum seekers are coming from and assess the statements they make. They cooperate with the Integration Agency and the Customs. They are responsible for asylum seekers until they enter the country. During the period in which asylum seekers benefit from asylum, the Ministry of Integration is responsible for them. The Ministry of Integration regularly issues reports on the capacities available for taking in asylum seekers.

Chapter 19: Integration

The Ministry of Integration is tasked with ensuring that the population is as peaceful and friendly as possible and with creating areas for protecting minorities.

Immigration is used to offset the birth rate so that full employment is guaranteed. In the short term, foreigners from outside the Continental Union will no longer be allowed to settle until all hereditary enmities between continental peoples have been eliminated. Foreigners will emigrate until the quota for foreigners is met. In the medium term, the continent opens up to immigration so that the quotas for foreigners are complied with in the member states. In the long term, no more borders exist anywhere in the world. The municipalities control the influx autonomously and report on local cultural groups or exclude themselves by establishing a cultural protection area.

Citizenship and aliens law lay down obligations for acquiring civil rights. Nationals receive their citizenship at birth if both parents are nationals. Children where only one parent is a nationals may choose one of their parents' nationalities until they come of age. Nationals do not hold any other nationality. Nationals have full voting, electoral and residence rights as nationals of their state. Postal voting is not offered to nationals who live abroad, although they are allowed to borrow their right to vote.

Foreigners are allowed to reside in the country as tourists, guests or naturalised foreigners. Tourists cannot be issued work permits. Guests can be issued with a work permit if a national enterprise recruits them because of a shortage of skilled workers. Tourists and guests need to obtain a visa from the embassy in their home country and receive a residence permit limited to a maximum of 10 years. This only becomes permanent through naturalisation. Guests who in the naturalisation test can demonstrate adequate knowledge of the national language, work ethic, virtue, religious belief, past of the country, loyalty to the constitution, respect for criminal law, basic arithmetic, writing and reading skills, and have passed the final examination in civil defence and fulfil all conditions of the naturalisation phase can be naturalised. Those who fail the test more than 3 times must leave the country within 12 months or are deported. The naturalisation period lasts a maximum of 10 years. Anyone who does not have at least 10 native friends by then, has not been a member of a club for at least 12 months, has never performed honorary work for at least a total of 2 months, does not speak the national language fluently, is in debt or has committed a criminal offence cannot be naturalised. Foreigners who become delinquent or insolvent are expelled and deported. The **Residents' Registration Office** is responsible for counting the population, issuing identity cards and ensuring freedom of settlement for all nationals. Foreigners can only settle where the quota of foreigners allows them to do so. **Identity cards** contain personal data such as face, fingerprints, iris, signature, name, first name, date of birth, place of birth, nationality, eye colour, height, address and ID card number. The card's title indicates the status of the holder. ID cards can also be used as People's Bank cards, Health Cards and intranet access cards. Nationals are issued with a national ID card that provides all voting rights for the voting machines and a passport. Children receive a child's ID card, which doubles as the People's Bank card to receive child benefit. Asylum seekers and refugees are issued with an asylum card showing their country of origin. Guests are issued with a guest card showing their nationality and date of departure. Naturalised foreigners are issued with a foreign citizen identity card showing their nationality. If they are shown to be delinquent or insolvent, they have to hand it in.

The **Integration Agency** is responsible for arrivals, immigration, emigration and deportation, records the grounds for these, measures their number and the quota of foreigners, liaises with other ministries, cultural and religious communities, maintains Integration Offices in the town halls and delivers integration measures.
Integration means adapting to each other and assimilation means adapting to the circumstances. Municipalities indicate whether they want newcomers to integrate or to assimilate.

Any language can be spoken, but with state employees, the national language has to be spoken or written. Those who are unable have to provide the appropriate translation. Women of childbearing age decide whether the population shrinks, stays the same or grows with their birth rate. At a birth rate of 2.1, the population remains the same, above that it grows, below that it shrinks. In order to involve men in this decision, the people vote on the terms of immigration and the quota of foreigners. If the people want the population to shrink, the quota of foreigners is lowered, if they want it to grow, the birth rate is increased. Native women are then asked whether and what political reasons there might be for the low birth rate. If the main reasons are personal, only single foreign women of childbearing age are allowed to immigrate.

In **Cultural protection area**s, minorities such as subcultures or extremists can exclude themselves from the majority. The constitution and the monopoly on the use of force of the Ministries of Security and Justice apply everywhere. Freedom of movement can be restricted to transit only and freedom to settle can be withdrawn altogether. At least 75 per cent of the citizens of a municipality can table an initiative to establish a cultural protection area in order to enact the new municipal laws in a committee, which have to be approved by at least 90 per cent of the inhabitants of the municipality. These rules will be posted on the town limits sign and published on the intranet. Those who break these rules will receive a warning or be banned, which can be indefinite and extended to the entire cultural protection area. Physical, material and financial integrity remains intact. A majority of at least 65 per cent of the people can dissolve cultural protection areas if danger threatens, but must leave the minority with at least one town as a cultural protection area.

Only **Religious communities** that are loyal to the constitution are approved. These are obliged to have their pastors trained in state colleges and pay for the necessary teaching posts. They can have their church tax collected through the People's Bank. They are allowed to establish places of worship that are open to everyone, where preaching and prayer take place in the national language and where the national constitution is available for viewing. Several religious communities are reconciled with one another. State and church are kept separate. Separate church laws, courts or labour unions are not permitted; all democratically enacted state laws and the state's monopoly on the use of force apply. Crimes committed in religious communities are punished by the state. Religious communities which break the law can be banned from practising, their places of worship can be closed or the religious communities can be dismantled.

Immigration is controlled by imposing a time limit on residency, charging entrance fees, ending permanent residency when there is evidence of crime and excessive debt, and by placing quotas on foreigners to prohibit immigration or make deportation necessary. Foreigners are only allowed to rent or lease land. The naturalisation phase is waived for citizens of Continental Union member states and a higher quota of foreigners applies. The visa requirement is waived for foreigners of states which the country has a corresponding agreement with. All citizens of other states require a visa. If complaints occur between nationals and foreigners, the integration authority convenes an integration committee where the disputes are settled. In the vote on the **Quota of foreigners**, nationals indicate whether foreigners should integrate or assimilate, whether immigration should be linked to full employment and how many foreigners, asylum seekers and refugees should be allowed to live in their community and in the country as a whole compared to the national population. The maximum limit is represented by the quota for the whole country of 20 per cent Continental Union citizens and 5 per cent other foreigners. Immigration is halted when unemployment reaches 1 per cent. Before entering the country, foreigners indicate whether they want to settle in the country or return to their home country and whether they want to integrate or assimilate. The Integration Agency and Integration Directory resolve problems of distribution issues between municipalities. **Immigration conditions** are different for asylum seekers, guest workers and other immigrants. However, across all categories, immigrants do not have a criminal record and can support themselves and, if necessary, their families. Guest workers and other immigrants also need savings of $20,000 or more. The Free Market Economy also requires a deposit of $20,000, the Social Market Economy a payment of $200,000, the Planned Economy $1,000,000 and the Barter Economy $500,000 to adjust their capacities accordingly. The wage for guest workers is 30 per cent higher than standard in the Social Market Economy and 10 per cent higher in the Free Market Economy. Guest work becomes illegal when the unemployment rate exceeds 3 per cent and is not allowed in the Planned Economy and Barter Economy. Export duties are levied on remittances sent abroad by foreigners to compensate for the loss of purchasing power. Immigration should take place for love of country and people, not for need. Foreigners must register for the **Immigration procedure** at the embassy in their home country. They submit their data there and look for a place to live and a job. The embassy checks whether all the conditions are met, compiles all the data required for an identity card and sends it to the Residents' Registration Office. Foreigners can then enter the country and have 3 months to find work and accommodation in order to receive their Guest ID card.

At the Integration Office, new arrivals receive information about the city and a guided tour. Newly arriving nationals and Continental Union citizens can and other foreigners must take part in **Integration measures** including language classes, visits from honorary nationals, immigrant festivals, theatre classes and bus trips to clubs, voluntary services and restaurants. In the civil defence course, they learn how to interact successfully with the public, learn how to protect their fellow human beings, and shadow the People's Protection Service for 3 months. The **Integration Directory** provides a digital overview of the quotas of foreigners, integration or assimilation in cities and characteristics of nationals. Those who want to move, immigrate or volunteer can create a profile and set up or find groups offering integration events. **Departure procedures** can be voluntary or forced. Anyone is allowed to leave as long as by doing so they do not attempt to avoid prosecution. If the quota of foreigners is exceeded, a sufficient number of foreigners need to emigrate voluntarily which they agree democratically among themselves. If not enough foreigners agree, first guests, then asylum seekers, refugees and finally naturalised foreigners are asked to return. Foreigners who are indebted are required to leave the country within 3 months. Foreigners who refuse to leave are deported. Foreigners with criminal convictions are also deported immediately after serving their sentence and are banned from entering the country for life. Those who are found to have violated the entry ban are imprisoned for 10 years. If foreigners are minors at the time of the offence, they are deported with their entire family. The foreigners have to pay for the deportation costs themselves. Those who are unable to pay first have to work them off in detention. Deportations are accompanied and enforced by Customs. Readmission is agreed, but if a country refuses to take in its own nationals, they are flown in by drones. Stateless persons are not allowed to enter. If they do, they commit a crime and are deported. Biometric data and genetic tests are used by the Integration Agency in tandem with embassies to determine possible country of origin of the person or their parents. The countries concerned receive the data and are expected to check whether they have already issued a passport or identity card to such persons. These persons are then deported to the respective country.

The reception capacities for **Asylum** seekers are determined by a People's Committee, who then receive permission to enter from the embassy. The Asylum Directory is used for collecting data about asylum seekers and for distributing and networking them, and is also available on the Internet. Initial reception takes place in the asylum-seekers' house in a Social Village. There, asylum seekers decide whether they want to be naturalised as refugees in a domestic host family environment or return to their country of origin following their period of asylum and move into an Asylum Village until then. Asylum Villages are built by asylum seekers in areas of the country where housing is scarce. They live, learn and work there until the Asylum Village is built and their country of origin is safe again. Asylum Villages are organised in the same planned way as Social Villages, so that asylum seekers can support themselves. However, the educational programmes are limited to basic care, housebuilding and political education. Companies exclusively offer the basic supply as well as the provision of building materials and construction machinery. They trade in a cryptocurrency in the Asylum Village and invest their entire assets in real estate bonds. These real estate bonds cover the construction costs for Asylum Villages. The buildings in the Asylum Villages are sold to nationals after the asylum seekers have left. The real estate bonds are then repaid to the asylum seekers together with interest. After their return, they are richer than before. Asylum seekers are only accommodated in the initial reception and in an Asylum Village with asylum seekers who speak the same language and who, if possible, come from the same region. Skilled workers can, however, be divided into Asylum Villages where they are missing. As a result, asylum seekers are able to quickly and successfully rebuild their country after their return, and they make the right contacts for this in the Asylum Village. Criminal asylum seekers are deported.

Chapter 20: Family

The task of the Ministry of Family Affairs is to ensure that the population can live together familial, peacefully and democratically. To this end, it works with the Ministries of Education, Infrastructure and the Planned Economy, as well as with clubs, youth centres and retirement homes. In order to ensure peaceful coexistence, the Ministry of Family Affairs enacts laws for **Manners**, which describe the personal and collective moral responsibility in dealing with one another.

In order to ensure democratic coexistence, the Ministry of Family Affairs issues laws to measure and favour the **Promotion of democracy** in the population and for equality and democratisation of all facilities for minors. The Youth Welfare Office oversees democratic coexistence in institutions that work with children.

The **Registry Office** supports citizens in matters of partnering, marriage, divorce and death with advice, documents, certifications and cure of souls.

Scientific research in these areas is carried out by the Institute for **Family** Research. The **Family Directory** is used for digital networking to find and meet friends, partners, adoptive children and adoptive parents. It also offers a digital platform for resolving disputes and for finding tips and courses for educational support.

Partnering means entering into and maintaining a sexual or love relationship. The regularisations concerning partnering describe how people can legally find partners for a love relationship or sexual relationship and what to look out for in certain relationships. The rules legalise love and sex across all genders and for any number of people. Phrases, gestures and digital or official consent are used to provide a legal way to find partners. A distinction is made between love and sex, so that people make their intentions known to each other before becoming partners. The Ministry of Family Affairs supports single people in finding a partner through events and suggestions for events. The parties are free to use other methods to find partners, but they run the risk that love or sex can lead to a criminal offence being committed, because the other person misunderstands ambiguous overtures or denies consent after the fact. As long as everyone acts with mutual consent, everything is permissible that does not harm any uninvolved parties. **Minors** may partner with each other from the age of 10, subject to a maximum age difference of 3 years. Partnerships between minors and adults is permitted only with an age difference of no more than 3 years.

Marriage is for the purpose of providing binding family support between the spouses and their children. The gender or number of spouses does not matter, only the age of majority. The marital relationship need not necessarily be based on love or sex, but can also be a friendly or neighbourly relationship. What the spouses stipulate in their marriage contract when they marry is decisive. The Ministry of Family Affairs puts forward suggestions that apply as long as the spouses do not change them by mutual agreement. The marriage contract regulates the choice of married name, joint or separate property, assets and insurance. If the marriage ends up in divorce, child support and the distribution of child custody and inheritance are also regulated. This makes court proceedings when a divorce takes place the exception.

The partners communicate their **Desire to have children** before sexual intercourse takes place. Otherwise, it is assumed that contraceptives will be used. In situations where they are unable to conceive, parents-to-be can resort to artificial insemination, women to sperm donations and sperm banks, men to surrogate mothers and surrogate mother databases. Fathers are not allowed to take drugs three months before and mothers during pregnancy and breastfeeding. Parents must obtain a parenting licence during pregnancy at the latest. The Registry Office checks parenting licences before issuing the birth certificate. If neither parent can produce a parenting licence, the family is accommodated in the Social Village until the tests have been completed. Youth Welfare Office staff visit new-borns once a month until they are three months old. Parental leave amounts to 12 months for each parent as unpaid leave with subsequent employment guarantee.

The **Youth Welfare Office** is responsible for all minors and ensures that parents and persons working with children look after the best interests of the child. Paediatricians, staff from educational institutions, the police and the Social Villages support them in this. If a child's welfare is placed in danger, penalties for parents and measures for children follow. In the worst case, children are relocated to the children's house in the Social Village and the parents are taken into prison. Children and parents can approve adoption and following mutual agreement mediation between adoptive children and adoptive parents takes place.

The **Parenting licence** serves to assure **Parenting** in favour of the child's rights. Parents can attend the courses in person or online or register directly for the final exam. The exam consists of a test and a self-written parenting guide. It can be repeated as often as required. The courses focus on the first two years of life and the lessons consist mainly of case studies and role play. This includes modes of behaviour during discussion, arguments, changing nappies and bodily discovery. Foreigners must have passed the parenting test no later than 9 months after immigration.

Children have a right to stable loving relationships, physical integrity and safety, individual testing of their talents, experiences appropriate to their developmental stage, equitable boundaries and structure, stable and supportive communities, and a viable humanity. The Youth Welfare Office provides the child emergency hotline for children who feel that their rights have been violated. To ensure that children can access their rights, they receive a Child ID card and child benefit paid into their child account at the People's Bank. Guardians are only allowed to use the child benefit to buy things for the child. Cash withdrawals are not allowed. To provide support growing up among peers, the Ministry of Family Affairs provides youth centres and the Youth Alliance for children and adolescents, which cooperates with various clubs and runs the youth fire brigade, scouts and organises tent camps for them. The youth centres house the municipal Youth Welfare Offices. The head office comprises a residential building including a dormitory, a parent-child room, a workshop and a stage area. The local centres are built by young people themselves in the forest or they are given old construction trailers or disused public transport vehicles. The duties of children and young people are regulated in the laws concerning the protection of minors and the age of majority. Curfews, bans on the purchase and consumption of drugs or dangerous and violence-glorifying products, and restrictions on business capacity, responsibility and liability are in place to protect minors. The age of majority is reached when turning 18 and from then on age restrictions no longer apply.

The Ministry of Family Affairs promotes **Leisure** activities by providing opportunities to pursue fine arts, drama, music and sports. It helps citizens to pursue recreational activities by providing equipment and licenses. It maintains playgrounds which offer something for all age groups and a traffic light system for noise abatement to protect residents. Furthermore, it provides donated toys as public property. The Ministry of Family Affairs sets guidelines for establishing and managing clubs and offers the Club Directory for this purpose. In the directory, offers can be posted, meetings arranged and opinions exchanged between members and other clubs, companies or state agencies. Honorary service providers can also use the Club Directory to organise themselves.

The Ministry of Family Affairs runs the Seniors' Alliance for **Senior citizens**, which organises assistance and leisure activities and supports seniors in founding and running retirement homes under their own responsibility.
The Ministry of Family Affairs regulates how **Death**s are dealt with. **Suicide** is permitted and can be carried out in the form of assisted suicide by volunteers or in person in suicide cells. Psychological and medical counselling and legal advice are provided in a series of three appointments prior to the suicide. Burial takes place in cemeteries. If cremation takes place, the ashes can be scattered anywhere where it does not harm anyone. The Ministry of Family Affairs maintains an archive of ancestors and settles inheritance issues. The Registry Office is also responsible for inheritance matters. It maintains a record of testaments. The Ministry of Family Affairs specifies who the testators and heirs are in a template of the testament, the order in which relatives inherit and how much their compulsory share is. In principle, testators have the right to modify the template made by the state according to their own wishes and are required have it certified digitally or in the Registry Office.

Charts

The following charts are described in Chapter 3 on State Organisation.

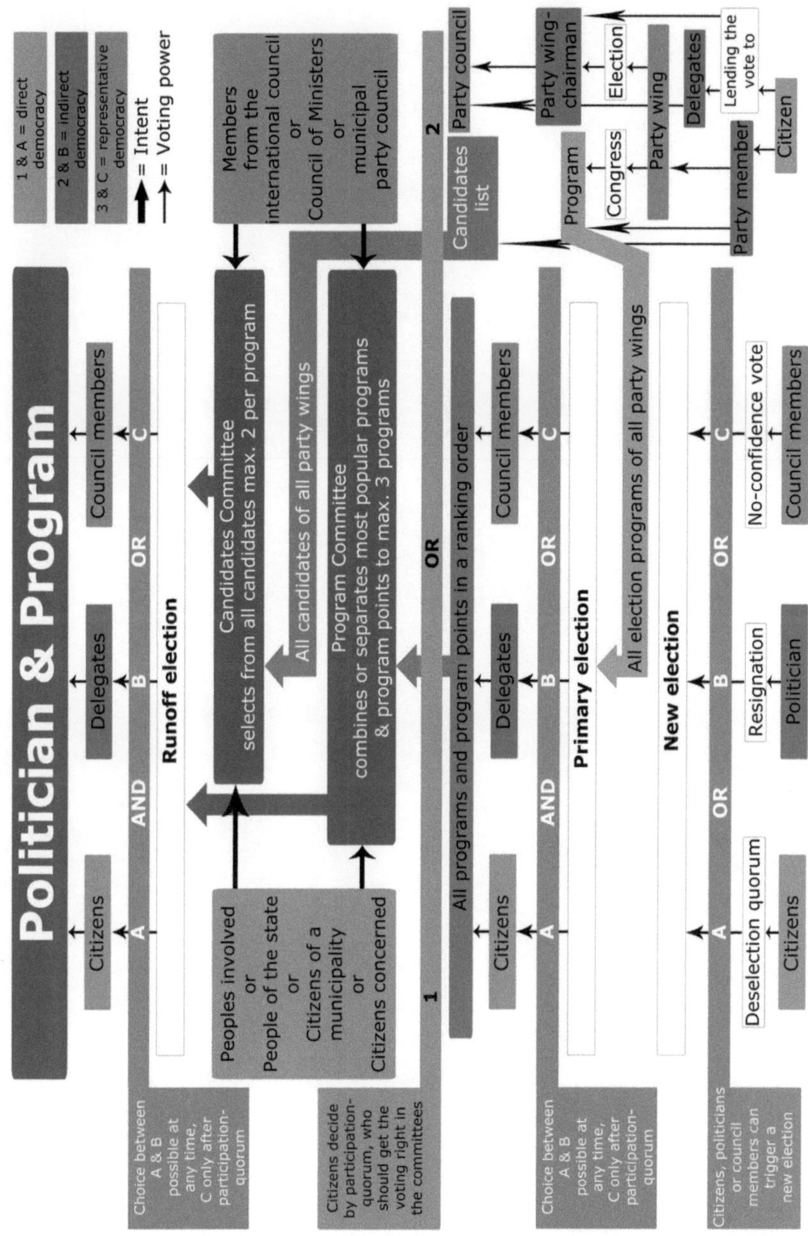

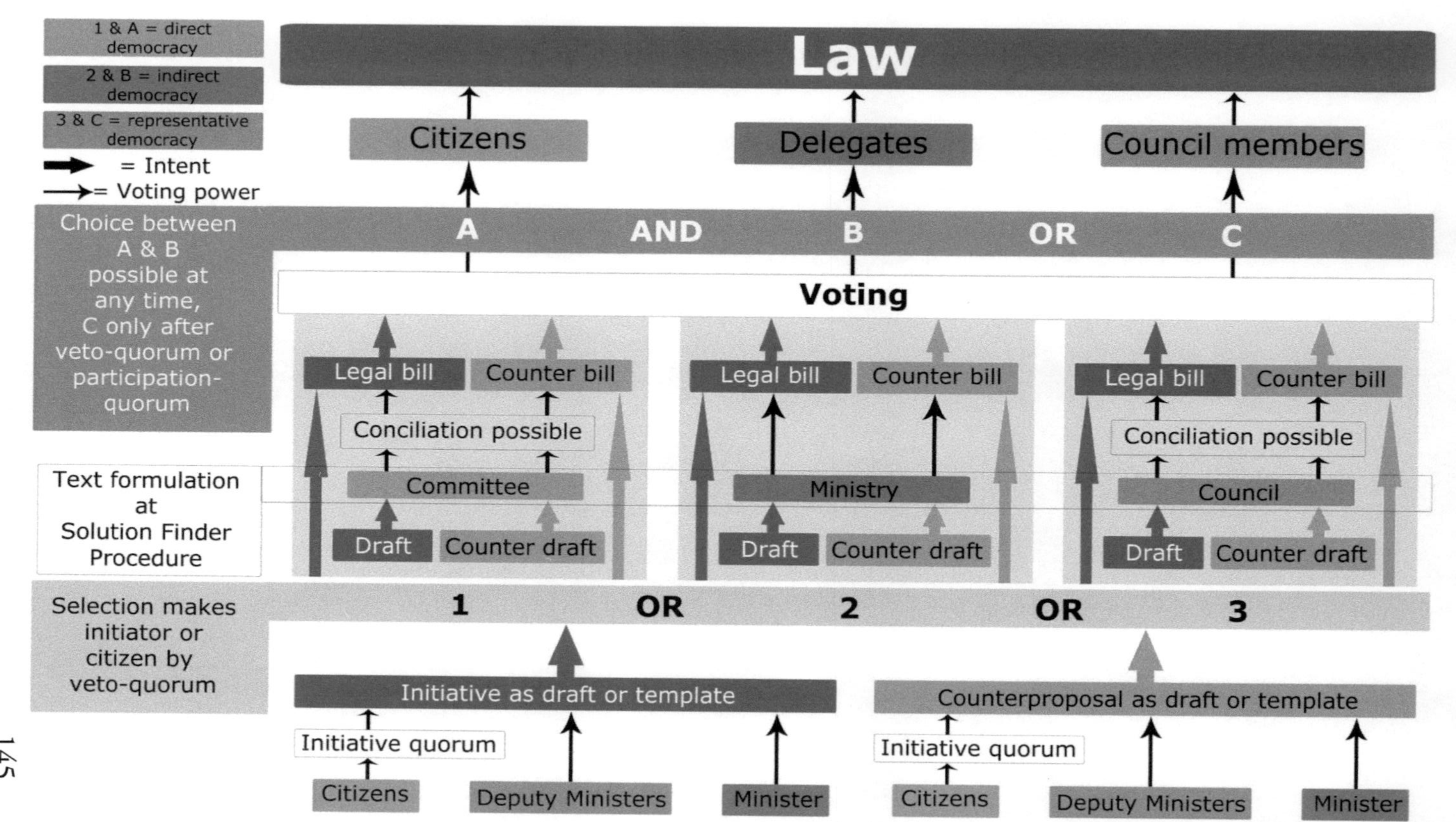
1 & A = direct democracy
2 & B = indirect democracy
3 & C = representative democracy
= Intent
= Voting power
Law
Citizens
Delegates
Council members
Choice between A & B possible at any time, C only after veto-quorum or participation-quorum
A
AND
B
OR
C
Voting
Legal bill
Counter bill
Conciliation possible
Committee
Text formulation at Solution Finder Procedure
Draft
Counter draft
Legal bill
Counter bill
Ministry
Draft
Counter draft
Legal bill
Counter bill
Conciliation possible
Council
Draft
Counter draft
Selection makes initiator or citizen by veto-quorum
1
OR
2
OR
3
Initiative as draft or template
Counterproposal as draft or template
Initiative quorum
Citizens
Deputy Ministers
Minister
Initiative quorum
Citizens
Deputy Ministers
Minister

Contact form

Dear reader
If you would like to make what you have read come true, in whole or in part, together with other like-minded people, I offer you several possibilities with this contact form. Fill it out, tear out the page and send it by post to:
Andreas Seidl, P.O. Box 1206, 63488 Seligenstadt / Germany

Or send the details to:
Phone: 0049 1522 818 2243 (whatsapp, telegram, signal)
Email: andreas.seidl2022@web.de

Please mark with a cross:
O   I want to found a dynamic People's Party.
O   I want to donate money for implementation.
O   I want contacts with like-minded people in my area.

Forename: ___________________________________

Surname: ___________________________________

Please fill in only the contact option through which a reply should be made.

Street, house no.:   _______________________________

Postcode, city, country: _________________________________

Phone: _______________________________

Email address: _______________________________